THE JEOPARDY!

·······►CHALLENGE◄·······

The Toughest Games from America's Greatest Quiz Show!

By the same authors

The Jeopardy! *Book*

THE JEOPARDY! CHALLENGE

The Toughest Games from America's Greatest Quiz Show!

FEATURING

- The Teen Tournament • The College Tournament
- The Seniors Tournament • The Tournament of Champions!

ALEX TREBEK & MERV GRIFFIN

HarperPerennial

A Division of HarperCollinsPublishers

THE *JEOPARDY!* CHALLENGE. Copyright © 1992 by Jeopardy Productions, Inc. All rights reserved. Printed in the United States of America. No part of this book may be used or reproduced in any manner whatsoever without written permission except in the case of brief quotations embodied in critical articles and reviews. For information address HarperCollins Publishers, Inc., 10 East 53rd Street, New York, NY 10022.

HarperCollins books may be purchased for educational, business, or sales promotional use. For information, please write: Special Markets Department, HarperCollins Publishers, Inc., 10 East 53rd Street, New York, NY 10022.

FIRST EDITION

Designed by C. Linda Dingler

Library of Congress Cataloging-in-Publication Data

Trebek, Alex, 1940–
  The Jeopardy! challenge / by Alex Trebek & Merv Griffin.—1st ed.
      p. cm.
    ISBN 0-06-096935-0 (pbk.)
    1. Questions and answers. 2. Jeopardy (Television program)—Miscellanea. I. Griffin, Merv.
II. Title.
  AG195.T74   1992
  031.02—dc20   92–52632

92 93 94 95 96 CC/RRD 10 9 8 7 6 5 4 3 2 1

Foreword

Merv Griffin

The first time I showed *Jeopardy!* to NBC it was titled *What's the Question?* I rented, for the day, a small theater in the Rockefeller Center complex that could handle the set we had built for an elaborate presentation . . . or so I thought!

We moved the set in on the morning of the audition with great effort. When we got the game board on the stage, it had to be put in sideways and still it hung over the lip of the stage and out over the first three rows. I had at least fifteen categories available to be played for the whole half-hour. The NBC execs had to sit over in one corner of the auditorium. It was a disaster. Their advice was to cut the board down into sections, as there was no way to photograph it for television.

Back to the office we went to attempt to break the show down into rounds. A daytime-TV exec named Ed Vane met with me and kept saying the show needed more jeopardies within the playing. I never heard another word he said. "Jeopardy" immediately became my mantra. I also kept thinking about a movie I liked titled *Double Jeopardy.* "Final Jeopardy" was then a natural bonus. We also added a feature, the "Daily Double," by which players could earn the right to double their monies. NBC hated the phrase, because it suggested racetrack gambling—a major no-no on TV. We fought and finally won that fight. We then went into new run-throughs with enthusiasm.

Our next presentation for NBC was totally different. We'd spent all our big bucks on the first theater run-through, so I suggested we take the ultimate leap and do it off the wall in the NBC boardroom.

We got a large piece of thick cardboard and wrote "Jeopardy" on it. I then took envelopes, cut the flaps off, and pasted them backward to the cardboard and inserted into each envelope a typewritten "answer." This was our game-board, which we glued to the expensive wall. We did the same for the "Double" and "Final" Jeopardies.

We found contestants and invited the Big Boss of NBC, Mort Werner, and his assistant, Grant Tinker (later to become one of TV's great executives as president of NBC), to be our audience. After emceeing the show for them, I looked at Mort Werner for his reaction. He looked at me without expression and said, "I didn't get *one.*" My heart sank. Grant Tinker said, "Buy it." Mort protested, "But I didn't get one question!" Grant repeated, "Buy it." And they did.

For the first few weeks of the show, my staff canvassed area colleges and Greenwich Village to find contestants. Many wore black capes on the show and looked unkempt, as intellectuals were supposed to. All I could think of were the many communists I kept seeing on the newscasts who were speaking out against America.

In the midst of all this, the head of NBC research arrived in my office with an easel and a lot of graphs, all of which indicated that if I didn't reduce the degree of difficulty in the game, the show would go off the air. He left, I never told anyone about his dire prophecy, and away we went.

Here we are, twenty-eight years later, tougher than ever, and still a major hit. You can question our answers, but don't ever question the intelligence of the audience.

Introduction

Alex Trebek

When I was asked to write an introduction to *The Jeopardy! Challenge,* I was delighted for two reasons. One, it means that the first book was a success and that people really enjoyed reading and learning more about our television show. Two, it gives me an opportunity to answer some questions that I was unable to address in the first *Jeopardy!* book.

In responding to the mail from our viewers, I have found that there are several areas that are asked about consistently. This is my chance to clear up some of those questions.

Who are all those people on stage during the commercial break that precedes Final Jeopardy!?

I know the set may look crowded at that moment, but those people are there for a reason. Two contestant coordinators assist the players in using the electronic pens so that the wagers are placed properly on the screens. Two production assistants record the wagers and transmit that information to our director and our computer operator so that when the responses are revealed we are able to display the updated scores immediately. A makeup man is there to wipe away any last-minute pressure perspiration, and a stage manager is present to tell everyone how much time is left before we come out of the commercial break.

Why does it seem that there are few minorities or women on the show?

We are always looking for good contestants of *all* types, and we do not discriminate on any basis. The reason you may see fewer players of a specific race or gender is that they simply do not try out in any great number, not because they do not make good players. Perhaps as we encourage more women and minority group members to try out, more of them will appear on the show. I would like to point out, in case you missed our 1992 Teen Tournament, all three finalists were girls.

How does someone try out for Jeopardy!?

We conduct contestant interviews throughout the year in Los Angeles, as well as searches in selected cities across the United States. Everyone who appears on *Jeopardy!* must take a fifty-question general knowledge exam. Those who pass the test then play a mock version of the game and are briefly interviewed. Players who qualify will be considered eligible for the current tape year, and may be scheduled for taping later that year. If they are not called to compete, we encourage them to reapply. One young man, who reapplied four times, wound up winning our College Championship. Since the test is difficult, we do not encourage anyone to come to Hollywood for the sole purpose of trying out for the show. If we are going to be in your area for a contestant search, it will be announced on the air by the local station that carries *Jeopardy!* Individuals who are under eighteen years of age or have been on any game show within the past year or on more than two game shows in the past five years are ineligible (the Teen Tournament, however, features thirteen- to seventeen-year-olds as contestants). Should you wish to come in for an interview, appointments can be made by calling our receptionist at (213) 466–3931 between the hours of 10:00 A.M. and 4:30 P.M. (Pacific Time).

Are contestants "matched" with categories according to their expertise?

Our contestants and the material that appears in any given show are chosen completely at random, without regard to each other. Because of this random selection, there may be times when, for example, we have a "Law" category on the show, as well as a contestant who happens to be a lawyer. However, when such an occasion arises, it is purely a coincidence. Precisely because the categories are randomly selected, it is difficult to continue as a champion for several days in a row. On any given day, the categories might favor one contestant over another, but the next show may be full of material about which the player knows relatively little.

When do the players make their Final Jeopardy! wagers?

After the Final Jeopardy! category is announced, there is a commercial break. During that break, the players write down their wagers, based on their knowledge of the category as well as their position in the competition. After the wagers are locked in, the Final Jeopardy! clue is revealed, and players have thirty seconds to write their responses. After the thirty seconds have elapsed, the electronic light pens (which, incidentally, are a bit difficult to operate, accounting for the poor penmanship of some of our contestants) cease to operate, and anything the player writes after that time will not be recorded.

Why do you punctuate differently from the way we were taught in school, with the quotation marks before a period or comma?

It is obvious that we do not agree with the convention to which you refer, which has been adopted in the United States primarily through the influence of printers and typesetters. Our original Editorial Associate Producer was the product of an English education, and he favored what he called a more "logical" approach to this matter. By punctuating in this manner, we feel our clues are less confusing, and because of the typeface which we use, easier to read.

Do you accept suggestions and material from viewers?

Unfortunately, for legal reasons, it is against company policy to accept any material from outside sources. That is a shame, because I'm sure that our viewers often have good ideas for clues or categories. Nevertheless, we have had to institute our "no submissions" policy, and in cases where a viewer does send in material, we return it without even looking at it.

Why don't the second- and third-place contestants get to keep the cash they've earned?

I dealt with this in *The Jeopardy! Book,* but for those of you who missed it, here it is again. We deliberately chose not to award the second- and third-place contestants cash in order to maintain what we hoped would be a good competition. Otherwise, we felt that with the large amounts of money available, contestants might choose to play conservatively in the Final Jeopardy! round and bet little or nothing to save their earnings up to that time. This would lessen the competition and excitement for the viewer during Final Jeopardy! We feel the choice has been justified, since the games have become extremely competitive, and viewers seem to enjoy the shows. Incidentally, the average value of the second-place prize is over $2,500, and the third-place prize averages just under $1,000.

Why is it that sometimes in the interview segment it seems that you talk to one player longer than the others?

When we tape the show, I make a point of talking to each of our players for about the same amount of time. However, on occasion, when our show runs too long, a portion of the program has to be edited. Since we cannot take out part of the actual game playing, our associate director is forced to edit out a portion of an interview. When this happens, the cut that is made is usually one that is technically easier but not always the best in terms of continuity. We try not to have this happen too often, but sometimes it becomes necessary.

Why do you not always cover all the clues available in a round?

Contrary to some viewers' perceptions, it is not because the show is too "chatty." Usually, when we are unable to clear the board in a round, it is because there was a greater-than-average number of incorrect responses given by our contestants, or clues to which they were unable to respond, so that I had to give the right response. Both situations take up time, which means less time is available to cover the remainder of the material on the board. In addition, some categories such as "Spelling" take longer than others to play. In our Tournaments when the players perform extremely well and give few incorrect responses, we routinely clear the board. However, on average, we cover around twenty-eight of the thirty clues available in any given round, so, by and large, we do get to most of the material in any show.

How well would you do on the show?

I used to feel that I could compete relatively well with our players. However, as the years have gone by, I feel that I have "missed a step," and the younger players on our show would cream me (except, of course, in the Seniors Tournament, for which I am eligible).

Looking over the games presented in this book, I am once again impressed by the variety of material that we use on the show and about which our contestants are so knowledgeable. It reminds me how difficult it is to become a *Jeopardy!* champion, and that such individuals are truly worthy of our praise and congratulations—they really know their stuff!

If, in reviewing the material we present here, you find that *you* know a great number of the correct responses, perhaps you should consider trying out for our show. It's as simple as calling our office at (213) 466–3931 and making an appointment. As I have said, we are always looking for great contestants, and who knows, maybe you have what it takes to become the next *Jeopardy!* champion!

Tournament of Champions #1

JEOPARDY!

JOURNALISM

The public may subscribe to this paper that features a daily transcript of the activities of Congress

This CBS newsman once petitioned Churchill to let him broadcast outdoors so people could hear the Blitz

Sime Silverman, editor of this weekly trade paper, coined the headline "Sticks Nix Hick Pix"

Born in Hungary, he ran the *St. Louis Post-Dispatch* before buying the *New York World*

UPI journalist who's the senior member of the White House press corps

CITY NICKNAMES

"The Big Apple"

"The Cradle of Texas Liberty"

"The Crescent City"

"Kodak City"

"The Athens of the South"

PHYSICAL SCIENCE

Every year Australia moves two inches away from this nearest U.S. state and Japan moves three inches closer

France derives a higher percentage of its electricity from this energy source than any other country

Carbohydrates, such as sugars and starch, contain these three elements

$-273.15°C$

A space telescope launched by the space shuttle in 1990 is named for this twentieth-century astronomer

U.S. HISTORY

Century in which the most states, 29, were admitted to the union

John Q. Adams and Henry Clay were among those who negotiated the Treaty of Ghent that ended this war

The first English settlement in Maine occurred in this same year as the settlement of Jamestown

This disease transmitted by the *aedes aegypti* mosquito was brought to America on slave ships

In 1954 he was elected to the Senate from South Carolina by a write-in vote

SINGERS

When he got his star on Hollywood's walk of fame, this Welshman tossed garters to his fans

Katey Sagal of "Married . . . with Children" used to be one of the Harlettes, who sang back-up for this star

He played a sleazy evangelist in the James Bond film *License to Kill*

Emmy-winning TV hostess whose hometown, Winchester, Tennessee, renamed its main street in her honor

This Aussie singer was once a commissioner of parks and recreation for the state of California

12-LETTER WORDS

From the Greek for "fire" and "craft," it's a fancy word for a fireworks display

Stereophonic times two

In other words this exclamation can be "violin bows!"

Kids could tell the post office the dinosaur called this on a stamp is actually an *apatosaurus*

Literary term for words like "hiss," "fizz," "kerflop," "kerplunk," and "kerflooey"

JEOPARDY!

JOURNALISM

What is the *Congressional Record?*

Who is Edward R. Murrow?

What is *Variety?*

Who was Joseph Pulitzer?

Who is Helen Thomas?

CITY NICKNAMES

What is New York City?

What is San Antonio?

What is New Orleans?

What is Rochester, New York?

What is Nashville?

PHYSICAL SCIENCE

What is Hawaii?

What is nuclear energy?

What are carbon, hydrogen, and oxygen?

What is absolute zero?

Who was Edwin Hubble?

U.S. HISTORY	SINGERS	12-LETTER WORDS
What is the nineteenth century?	Who is Tom Jones?	What is pyrotechnics?
What was the War of 1812?	Who is Bette Midler?	What is quadraphonic?
What is 1607?	Who is Wayne Newton?	What is "fiddlesticks!"?
What is yellow fever?	Who is Dinah Shore?	What is a brontosaurus?
Who is Strom Thurmond?	Who is Helen Reddy?	What is onomatopoeia?

DOUBLE JEOPARDY!

ABBREVIATIONS

Abbreviated "hdbk," a Boy Scout might consult one

Performing art in which you'd find abbreviations such as "sfz," "pp," and "ff"

The abbreviation for manager is "mgr," whereas "msgr" stands for this

If you reverse this month's three-letter abbreviation, you get the symbol of one of its astrological signs

Of the four main compass points, these three are also symbols of elements

SCOTLAND

This term for the extended family comes from the Gaelic for "children"

The Scots word for "twilight"; Sir Harry Lauder used to sing about "Roamin' in" it

Silly-sounding name for the estuary of the river Forth

Scotland's national flag displays the cross of this man, its patron saint

Range of hills that was home to Sir Walter Scott's *Bride* and Donizetti's *Lucia*

BALLET

Tamara Karsavina was the first to dance the role of this Stravinsky bird, in 1910

This Dame, born Margaret Hookham, has been called "the greatest British ballerina of all time"

A "battement" is this specific movement, and can be high or low

Mental illness ended his career after he choreographed his last ballet, "Till Eulenspiegel"

Balanchine's ballet "Le Bourgeois Gentilhomme" is based on a seventeenth-century play by this Frenchman

MEDICINES	POETRY	FAMOUS EDUCATORS
Dramamine or Phenergan taken about one-half hour before traveling will help prevent this	Five-line humorous verse named for an Irish county	Preschool education method named for the Italian woman who originated it in 1907
Miles Laboratories has been selling this analgesic antacid tablet since 1931	His poem "Mending Wall" first appeared in *North of Boston,* a collection of poems he wrote in England	In 1925 this Dayton, Tennessee, biology teacher was arrested for teaching evolution in his class
On March 20, 1987, this drug became the first approved by the FDA for use in combating the AIDS virus	Not only did he write *Don Juan,* he proved it was possible to swim the Hellespont by doing it himself	Both John R. Gregg and Sir Isaac Pitman are famous for developing and teaching systems of this
In 1988 this prescription acne cream was found to reverse the effects of sun-induced wrinkles	He wrote, "I hope to see my pilot face to face when I have crost the bar"	This Swiss child psychologist was a professor at the University of Geneva from 1929 until his death in 1980
First used for high blood pressure, this drug, the key ingredient in Rogaine, can stimulate hair growth	In "The Baite" he wrote, "Come live with mee, and bee my love"	Though it caused much indignation in the south, Teddy Roosevelt invited this educator to the White House

7

DOUBLE JEOPARDY!

ABBREVIATIONS	SCOTLAND	BALLET
What is a handbook?	What is clan?	What is "The Firebird"?
What is music?	What is the gloamin'?	Who is (Dame) Margot Fonteyn?
What is monsignor? (ACC: messenger)	What is the Firth of Forth?	What is a kick?
What is March?	Who is St. Andrew?	Who was (Vaslav) Nijinsky?
What are N, W, and S?	What are the Lammermoors?	Who was Molière?

MEDICINES	POETRY	FAMOUS EDUCATORS
What is motion sickness?	What is Limerick?	What is the Montessori Method? (for Maria Montessori)
What is Alka-Seltzer?	Who is Robert Frost?	Who was John T. Scopes?
What is AZT? (azidothymidine)	Who was Lord Byron?	What is shorthand (stenography)?
What is Retin-A?	Who is Alfred (Lord) Tennyson?	Who was Jean Piaget?
What is Minoxidil?	Who was John Donne?	Who was Booker T. Washington?

FINAL JEOPARDY!

FICTIONAL CHARACTERS

Hired as a ship's cook, he led the mutiny aboard the *Hispaniola*

FINAL JEOPARDY!

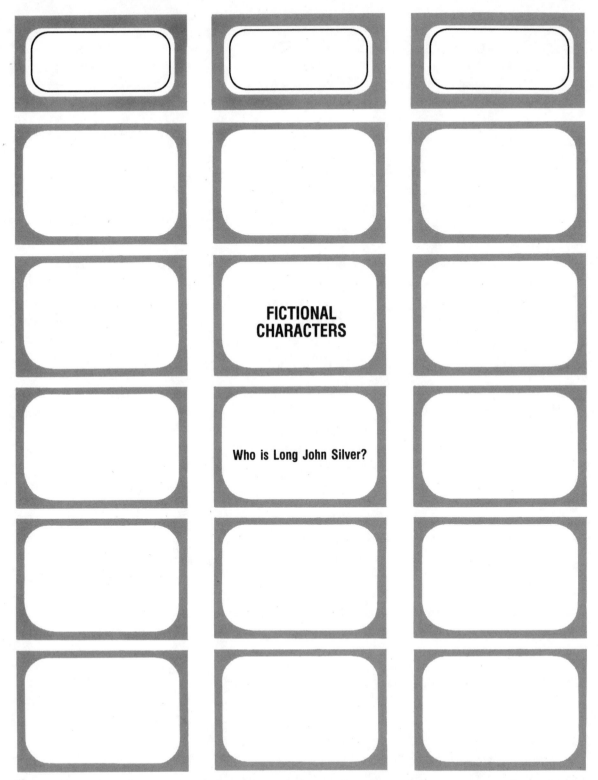

FICTIONAL CHARACTERS

Who is Long John Silver?

Tournament of Champions #2

JEOPARDY!

WORD ORIGINS

"Saloon" came from this French word, which sounds much more elegant

Shade of purple whose name comes from a word for mallow because it's the color of mallow petals

Derived from the Greek for "to sell alone," if you have one, you alone sell a product

The "chop" in "chopsticks" means this in pidgin English, as in "chop-chop"

This synonym for "gloomy" comes from a Medieval Latin term for "evil days"

WOMEN IN SPORTS

In 1989 12-year-old Victoria Brucker became the first U.S. girl to play in this baseball event

This runner who married Richard Slaney in 1985 holds six U.S. records, from 800 meters to 10,000 meters

The first Olympic marathon for women was won by this American in 1984

In 1979 Ann Meyers became the first woman to sign with a men's team in this pro sport

The first American woman to win the world title in this sport was Tenley Albright

NUCLEAR PHYSICS

Pu doesn't refer to the smell of a reactor but to this fuel in it

This element, assigned atomic mass unit of 12,000, is the standard from which others are measured

In nuclear fission mass from the neutron and the bombarded nucleus become energy as per this equation

Term for the least amount of fuel needed to keep up a chain reaction in a reactor

J. J. Thompson developed a cathode-ray tube with a screen to measure velocity of these particles

TELEVISION

This $104 million sequel to "The Winds of War" had 358 speaking parts and used 41,720 extras

Co-executive producer of "The Mary Tyler Moore Show," he later produced *Terms of Endearment*

Of "Rhoda," "Riptide," or "Remington Steele," the one that starred the daughter of a famous actor

The Robinsons, Don West, the robot, and this cowardly doctor were "Lost in Space"

A year before "Matt Houston," he was Archie Goodwin on "Nero Wolfe"

GOVERNMENT & POLITICS

He was the first living president to appear on U.S. paper money—on a $10 demand note authorized in 1861

In 1988 this Democrat was re-elected to the U.S. Senate from Texas

The Constitution originally held that untaxed members of this ethnic group were not to be counted in the census

The Office of Registrar of Copyrights is a division of this library

As this president's treasury secretary, Henry Morgenthau supervised the spending of some $370 billion without scandal

"C" IN GEOGRAPHY

The name of two cities, one in England and one in the U.S., both famous for their universities

This city was founded by England's East India Trading Company in 1690

American city that's served by the Kennedy, Eisenhower, Stevenson, and Dan Ryan expressways

Dalmatia, for which a dog breed is named, is part of this republic of Yugoslavia

Picturesque Ionian island that was the birthplace of Britain's Prince Philip

JEOPARDY!

WORD ORIGINS

What is salon?

What is mauve?

What is a monopoly?

What is fast?

What is dismal?

WOMEN IN SPORTS

What is the Little League World Series?

Who is Mary Decker?

Who is Joan Benoit (Samuelson)?

What is basketball?

What is figure skating?

NUCLEAR PHYSICS

What is plutonium?

What is carbon?

What is $E = MC^2$?

What is the critical mass?

What are electrons?

TELEVISION

What is "War and Remembrance"?

Who is James L. Brooks?

What is "Remington Steele"?

Who was Dr. Zachary Smith?

Who is Lee Horsley?

GOVERNMENT & POLITICS

Who was Abraham Lincoln?

Who is Lloyd Bentsen?

Who were Indians?

What is the Library of Congress?

Who was FDR?

"C" IN GEOGRAPHY

What is Cambridge?

What is Calcutta?

What is Chicago?

What is Croatia?

What is Corfu?

DOUBLE JEOPARDY!

RULERS

England's Alfred was the Great; Scotland's Robert I was this

Russia's Catherines I and II were married to men with this first name

When Napoleon put him on Spain's throne, California also came under his rule

From 1644–1912 this group of people ran the Ch'ing Dynasty in China

In the fifteenth century the Attendoli family came to rule Milan and changed its name to this, meaning "force"

TIME

It's how long "I've been working on the railroad"

The first month of the year with just 30 days in it

In the Queen's English, the phrase "Time, gentlemen, please!" refers to this

By the end of this era, the last trilobite bit the dust and all we have are fossil memories

The Muslim calendar reckons time from this event

PLAYWRIGHTS

Marsha Mason starred in his comedy *The Good Doctor,* based on stories by Chekhov

His first two produced plays were *The Zoo Story* and *The Death of Bessie Smith*

Francis Beaumont began his famous collaboration with this man around 1608

In 1952 she told the HUAC, "I cannot and will not cut my conscience to fit this year's fashions"

After writing *The School for Scandal,* he became an M.P. and an advisor to the future King George IV

THE PACIFIC ISLANDS

The Paul Gauguin Museum on this island where he lived in the 1890s owns no original paintings

The eastern part of this island group is American; the western part an independent country

Associated with New Zealand, these South Sea islands named for an explorer are self-governing

Belgian priest Father Damien ministered to the lepers on this Hawaiian island

Following a 1987 military coup, this island country quit the British Commonwealth

BIBLICAL QUOTES

"There hath not come a razor upon mine head, for I have been a Nazarite unto God," he told Delilah

"To every thing there is" this, "and a time to every purpose under the heaven"

"For what shall it profit a man if he shall gain the whole world and lose" this

In the 23rd Psalm, David referred to these two items of God's, saying "they comfort me"

"Now" this "is the substance of things hoped for, the evidence of things not seen"

OXFORD UNIVERSITY

You might call this Oxford graduate the "colossus of scholarships"

Some say Oxford was founded after this French university barred the English from attending

He was a fellow of Lincoln College, Oxford, when he co-founded Methodism with his brother Charles

He was expelled from Oxford but nevertheless learned 25 languages and translated *The Arabian Nights*

This cardinal, a dominant force during Henry VIII's reign, founded Oxford's Christ Church College

DOUBLE JEOPARDY!

RULERS	TIME	PLAYWRIGHTS
What was the Bruce?	What is "all the livelong day"?	Who is Neil Simon?
What is Peter?	What is April?	Who is Edward Albee?
Who was Joseph Bonaparte?	What is the pub (or bar) is about to close?	Who was (John) Fletcher?
Who were the Manchus?	What is the Paleozoic Era?	Who was Lillian Hellman?
What is Sforza?	What is the Hegira (Muhammad's flight)?	Who was (Richard Brinsley) Sheridan?

THE PACIFIC ISLANDS	BIBLICAL QUOTES	OXFORD UNIVERSITY
What is Tahiti?	Who was Samson?	Who was (Cecil) Rhodes?
What is Samoa?	What is "a season"?	What is (the University of) Paris?
What are the Cook Islands?	What is "his (own) soul"?	Who was John Wesley?
What is Molokai?	What are "Thy rod and thy staff"?	Who was (Sir Richard) Burton?
What is Fiji?	What is "faith"?	Who was (Thomas) Wolsey?

FINAL JEOPARDY!

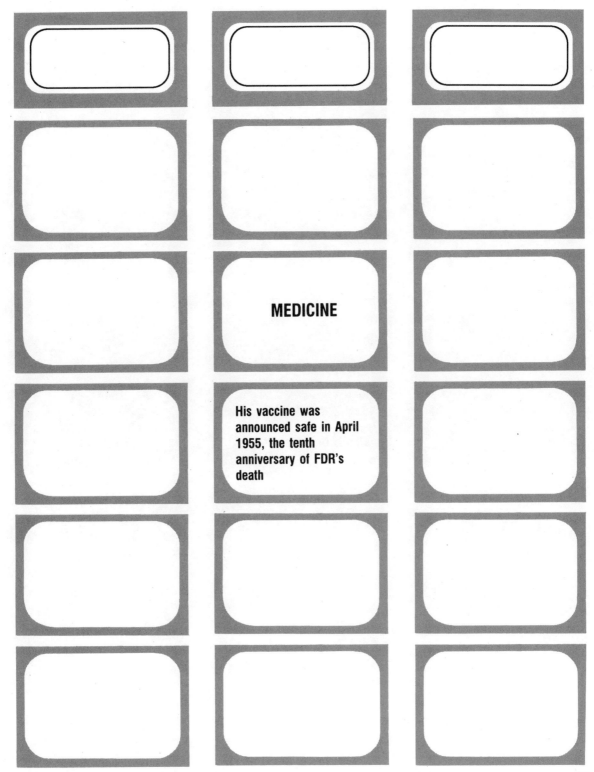

MEDICINE

His vaccine was announced safe in April 1955, the tenth anniversary of FDR's death

FINAL JEOPARDY!

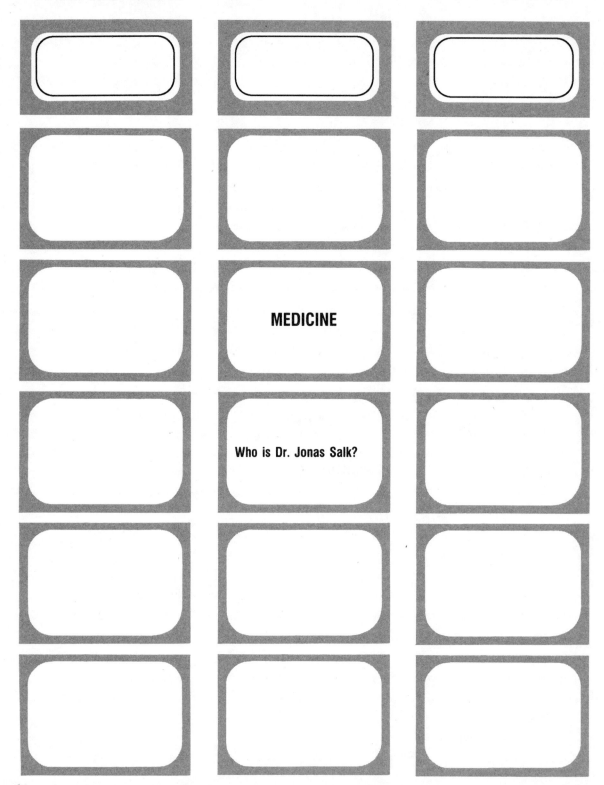

MEDICINE

Who is Dr. Jonas Salk?

Tournament of Champions #3

JEOPARDY!

PRESIDENTS

He once said, "I have never given anybody hell. I just tell the truth . . . and they think it's hell"

Showing he'd rather switch than fight, this future president changed from Democrat to Republican in 1962

At the shooting his assassin cried, "I am a stalwart and Arthur is president now!"

Shortly after being elected, he submitted his resignation as president of Columbia University

Jefferson Davis was the son-in-law of this president who died in office

POTPOURRI

In 1988 officials in this country admitted they had printed false maps for years to fool enemies

Hannibal had 38 of these animals when he began crossing the Alps, but few survived the ice and snow

Imported into Brazil from Africa, these "killer" insects escaped the lab and bred with locals

The U.S. Army awarded 8,612 medals after this 1983 invasion, although fewer than 7,000 troops were there

Both the father and son of the Frankish leader Charles Martel were named this

NORSE MYTHOLOGY

Norsemen believed the universe was supported by a huge one of these of the ash variety

Norse legend says a snake coiled around the world and this God of the sky will someday kill each other

Odin rode an eight-legged one of these named Sleipnir

Sigurd, called the most important hero in Norse myth, is famous for killing Fafnir, one of these

Bifrost, the bridge that connected the earth with the home of the gods, was one of these

MATH	FOREIGN FILMS	13-LETTER WORDS

MATH	FOREIGN FILMS	13-LETTER WORDS
Of means, medians, and modes, the term that's often called the arithmetic average	1959 grand prize winner at Cannes, it set the legend of Orpheus and Eurydice during Carnival in Rio	Any ability or accomplishment that makes a person suitable for a particular position or task
Fraction that's equivalent to the infinite decimal .666666 . . .	Mel Gibson hit the road again in this first sequel to George Miller's *Mad Max*	Vaduz is the capital of this 62-square-mile principality nestled between Switzerland and Austria
His theorem is often expressed: $a^2 + b^2 = c^2$	Lina Wertmuller film in which Giancarlo Giannini plays a small-time hood with seven ugly sisters	To be of a contemplative turn of mind, like Hume or Whitehead
Its symbol is called a radical sign	Originally a Swedish mini-series, this Ingmar Bergman film was called *Scener ur ett aktenskap*	The *Book of Common Prayer* says the peace of God "passeth all" of this
Branch of math meaning "pebble" in Latin, it's also related to a word that means "to determine by math"	*Knife in the Water*, Roman Polanski's first feature film, was made in this language	The loss of water vapor from the surface of a plant, usually through open stomata

JEOPARDY!

PRESIDENTS	POTPOURRI	NORSE MYTHOLOGY
Who was Harry Truman?	What is the USSR?	What is a tree?
Who is Ronald Reagan?	What were elephants?	Who is Thor?
Who was James A. Garfield?	What are (Honey) bees?	What is a horse?
Who was Dwight D. Eisenhower?	What was Grenada?	What is a dragon?
Who was Zachary Taylor?	What is Pepin?	What is a rainbow?

MATH	FOREIGN FILMS	13-LETTER WORDS
What is mean?	What is *Black Orpheus?*	What is a qualification?
What is two-thirds?	What is *The Road Warrior?*	What is Liechtenstein?
Who is Pythagoras?	What is *Seven Beauties?*	What is philosophical?
What is a square root?	What is *Scenes from a Marriage?*	What is understanding?
What is calculus?	What is Polish?	What is transpiration?

DOUBLE JEOPARDY!

HAUTE CUISINE

This basic white sauce becomes Mornay sauce with the addition of cheese

You can't make a soufflé without breaking some eggs and doing this to them before beating

Type of Swiss cheese that's an important ingredient in fondues, gratins, and crepes

A pâté-like dish, or the name of the mold in which pâté is baked

The middle cut of a rib steak, it literally means "between two ribs"

SICKNESS & HEALTH

Snellen's chart is standard equipment for giving this type of test

Surgical instrument that's most similar to tweezers

Childhood viral disease that causes swelling of the parotid glands

The key ingredient in smelling salts, which are used to revive a person who has fainted

Overweight heavy snorers are prone to this disorder in which breathing stops for short periods

ANCIENT GEOGRAPHY

Carthage has almost been destroyed; you can find what's left of it in a suburb of this Tunisian capital

Cuzco, capital of the Incan empire, is still the capital of Cuzco province in this country

If you wanted to hang around at the site of Babylon's famous gardens, you'd now have to go to this country

The Pale and what was beyond it referred to the medieval dominions of England in this country

Alexander the Great led his troops as far east as the Hyphasis, now the Beas, river in this country

NEWSPAPERS

In 1868 the first edition of this annual reference book was published by the *New York World*

He founded America's first newspaper chain and later took on Roy Howard as a partner

USA Today is published in this state

Boston has three daily newspapers: the *Globe*, the *Herald*, and this one with a national circulation

This Little Rock newspaper is the oldest west of the Mississippi and serves the entire state

ORCHESTRA CONDUCTORS

In 1980 he became conductor of the Boston Pops

He became conductor of the Philadelphia Orchestra in 1938 and remained there for over four decades

NBC created an orchestra for this conductor in 1937, disbanding it upon his retirement 17 years later

Controversial conductor of the Berlin Philharmonic who died in July 1989

This Russian-born cellist, who won the Lenin Prize in 1969, also conducted the National Symphony Orchestra

NAME THAT POET

"Should auld acquaintance be forgot, and never brought to mind?"

"Of all sad words of tongue or pen, the saddest are these: 'It might have been!'"

"It was many and many a year ago, in a kingdom by the sea"

"Hail to thee, blithe spirit! Bird thou never wert"

"Earth, receive an honoured guest; William Yeats is laid to rest: let the Irish vessel lie emptied of its poetry"

DOUBLE JEOPARDY!

HAUTE CUISINE	SICKNESS & HEALTH	ANCIENT GEOGRAPHY
What is béchamel sauce?	What is an eye test?	What is Tunis?
What is separating them?	What is a forcep?	What is Peru?
What is Gruyère?	What is mumps?	What is Iraq?
What is a terrine?	What is ammonia?	What is Ireland?
What is entrecôte?	What is sleep apnea?	What is India?

NEWSPAPERS	ORCHESTRA CONDUCTORS	NAME THAT POET
What is the *World Almanac?*	Who is John Williams?	Who was Robert Burns?
Who was (Edward) Scripps?	Who was Eugene Ormandy?	Who was John Greenleaf Whittier?
What is Virginia?	Who was Arturo Toscanini?	Who was Edgar Allan Poe?
What is the *Christian Science Monitor?*	Who was Herbert von Karajan?	Who was Percy Bysshe Shelley?
What is the *Arkansas Gazette?*	Who is Mstislav Rostropovich?	Who was W. H. Auden?

FINAL JEOPARDY!

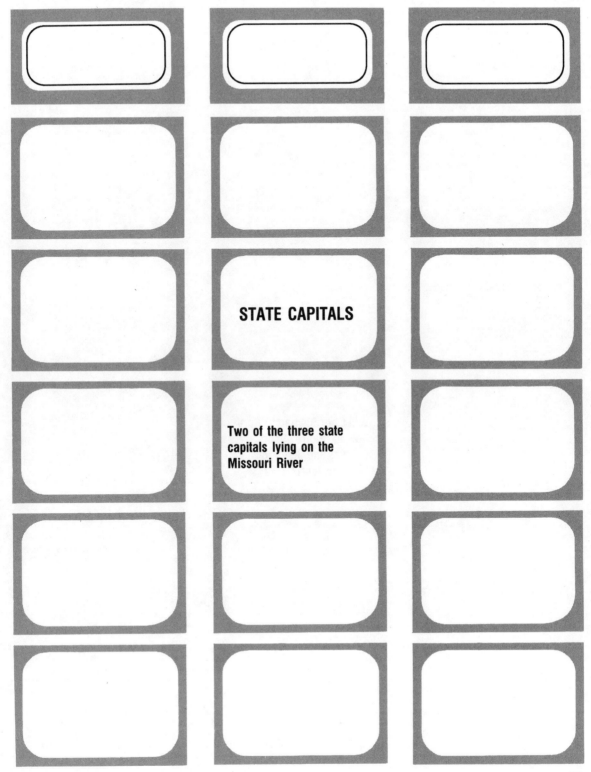

STATE CAPITALS

Two of the three state capitals lying on the Missouri River

FINAL JEOPARDY!

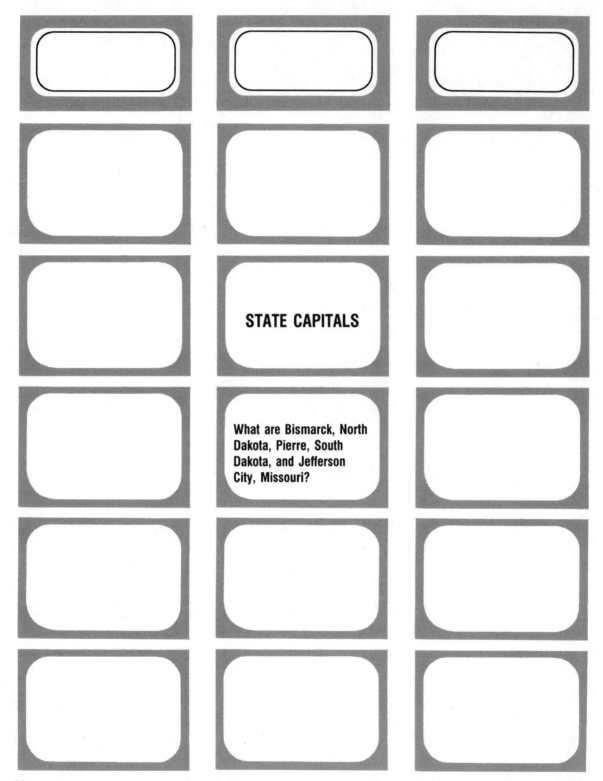

STATE CAPITALS

What are Bismarck, North Dakota, Pierre, South Dakota, and Jefferson City, Missouri?

Tournament of Champions #4

JEOPARDY!

CORPORATE AMERICA

To promote this park in San Antonio, Southwest Airlines painted a plane to resemble Shamu

Nabisco is hounding the bad doggie breath problem by adding this flavor to its Milk-Bones

The "al" in Alcoa stands for this

Automaker whose ad campaign centers around "The heartbeat of America"

According to *USA Today*, the five biggest corporate takeovers in U.S. history were in this industry

WOMEN IN WESTERNS

No more "Happy Trails" for her horse Buttermilk: he's stuffed in a museum

It was Grace Kelly's first, last, and only Western movie

In *The Searchers*, John Wayne searched for this actress

She played the mother of the little kid who yelled, "Come back! Shane!"

She fended off attacking Indians in *River of No Return*, with a little help from Robert Mitchum

ART

Term for Spain's Islamic art, it comes from the Muslim group that conquered the country in the eighth century

The starting point and center of early Renaissance art was in this Italian city

Many Rembrandt masterpieces hang in this "national museum" in Amsterdam

John Constable is best known for painting these

With works titled *White Line* and *Blue Segment*, this Russian has been called the first abstract painter

PATRON SAINTS

The name of this patron of wayfarers comes from Greek for "one who carries Christ"

Patron saint of children, his feast day is December 6, not December 25

Gospel writer who is the patron saint of Venice, his winged lion is the city's symbol

The family of this patron of students once kept him in a castle to keep him from becoming a friar

Called the apostle of organized charity, he's the patron of charitable societies

THE YEAR THAT WAS

An Orwell novel returned to the best-seller list, voters returned Reagan and Bush, "Jeopardy!" returned to TV

Anwar Sadat was shot, Pope John Paul II was shot, President Reagan was shot

China invaded Vietnam, the Soviets invaded Afghanistan, Iranians invaded the U.S. Embassy

The Bears won the Super Bowl, Elie Wiesel won the Nobel Peace Prize, Democrats won control of the U.S. Senate

Ford sent the Edsel to dealers, Ike sent troops to Little Rock, Russia sent Sputnik to space

ABBREV.

One of the two metal alloys abbreviated br.

A CEO whose company offers an EEO might hire some DAVs, who are these

States whose abbreviations make up the telegram:
HI PA.
MA OK.
AL

You gesture a lot but don't need to speak a word in this language, ASL

Two out of three federal workers might know that the BLS is this

JEOPARDY!

CORPORATE AMERICA	WOMEN IN WESTERNS	ART
What is Sea World?	Who is Dale Evans?	What is Moorish art?
What is mint?	What is *High Noon?*	What is Florence?
What is aluminum?	Who was Natalie Wood?	What is the Rijksmuseum?
What is Chevrolet?	Who is Jean Arthur?	What are landscapes?
What is oil?	Who was Marilyn Monroe?	Who was (Wassily) Kandinsky?

PATRON SAINTS	THE YEAR THAT WAS	ABBREV.
Who is St. Christopher?	What was 1984?	What is bronze or brass?
Who is St. Nicholas?	What was 1981?	What are Disabled American Veterans?
Who is St. Mark?	What was 1979?	What are Hawaii, Pennsylvania, Massachusetts, Oklahoma, Alabama?
Who was St. Thomas Aquinas?	What was 1986?	What is American sign language?
Who was St. Vincent de Paul?	What was 1957?	What is the Bureau of Labor Statistics?

DOUBLE JEOPARDY!

WORLD WAR I

American Doughboys called him "Kaiser Bill"

In 1917 the U.S. entered the war and this large country stopped fighting

The Allied Gallipoli campaign was beaten back by this country

The U.S. declared war on Germany April 6, 1917, and on this country the following December 7

A secret message from this German foreign secretary advocating a German-Mexican alliance angered the U.S.

LITERATURE

When he saw water snakes in the moonlight and blessed them, the albatross fell from his neck

He wrote his 1940 novel *The Naked and the Dead* while he was enrolled at the Sorbonne

She received the Pulitzer prize for her *Collected Stories*, not for *Ship of Fools*

The young narrator of *Treasure Island*

A well-known Ambrose Bierce short story is about an incident at this bridge in northern Alabama

ANATOMY

These body parts are sometimes called digits

One of the two hormones that regulate blood sugar in the pancreas

Otitis media is a term for infection of the middle part of this

Proper name for your shoulder blade

The connective tissue sac enclosing the heart

BROADWAY MUSICALS

In this show, the hero sells his soul to the Devil so the Washington Senators can win the Pennant

1776 climaxes with this historical event

Flo Ziegfeld was the original producer of this 1927 musical, which featured "Can't Help Lovin' Dat Man"

In April 1988 Phylicia Rashad took over Bernadette Peters' role as the witch in this Stephen Sondheim musical

Bonnie Franklin sang the title song in this 1970 musical starring Lauren Bacall

STATE CAPITALS

A library in this capital includes a near-complete collection of Kansas newspapers since 1875

It's the only one-word capital that has the name of its state contained within it

Southwest capital that is home of the Hall of Flame, the world's premier fire-fighting museum

One of two Confederate state capitals that Union troops did not capture during the Civil War

It replaced Guthrie in 1910, but it wasn't until 1923 that the post office officially recognized its name

"HUGH"'S & "HUGHES"

Robert Hughes hosted the first week of "20/20"; he took over on the second

This man, whose middle name was Robard, was played by Jason Robards in a 1980 film

1960 Spingarn medal winner, among this poet's works on his life in Harlem was "The Weary Blues"

He attended Rugby from 1834–42 and later set *Tom Brown's School Days* there

He became king of France in 987, beginning a dynasty of 14 kings

DOUBLE JEOPARDY!

WORLD WAR I	LITERATURE	ANATOMY
Who was Kaiser Wilhelm (II)? (ACC: William)	Who was the Ancient Mariner?	What are the fingers? (and the toes)
What was Russia (Soviet Union)?	Who is Norman Mailer?	What are glycogen and insulin?
What is Turkey?	Who was Katherine Anne Porter?	What is the ear?
What was Austria (-Hungary)?	Who is Jim Hawkins?	What is the scapula?
Who was (Arthur or Alfred) Zimmermann?	What is Owl Creek Bridge?	What is the pericardium?

BROADWAY MUSICALS	STATE CAPITALS	"HUGH"'S & "HUGHES"
What is *Damn Yankees?*	What is Topeka?	Who is Hugh Downs?
What is the signing of the Declaration of Independence?	What is Indianapolis?	Who was Howard Hughes?
What is *Show Boat?*	What is Phoenix?	Who was Langston Hughes?
What is *Into the Woods?*	What is Tallahassee or Austin?	Who was Thomas Hughes?
What is *Applause?*	What is Oklahoma City?	Who was Hugh Capet?

FINAL JEOPARDY!

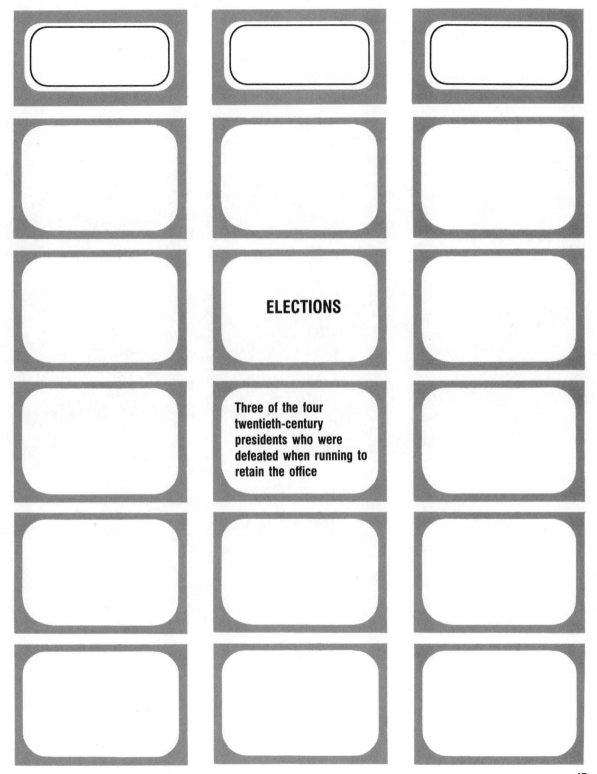

ELECTIONS

Three of the four twentieth-century presidents who were defeated when running to retain the office

FINAL JEOPARDY!

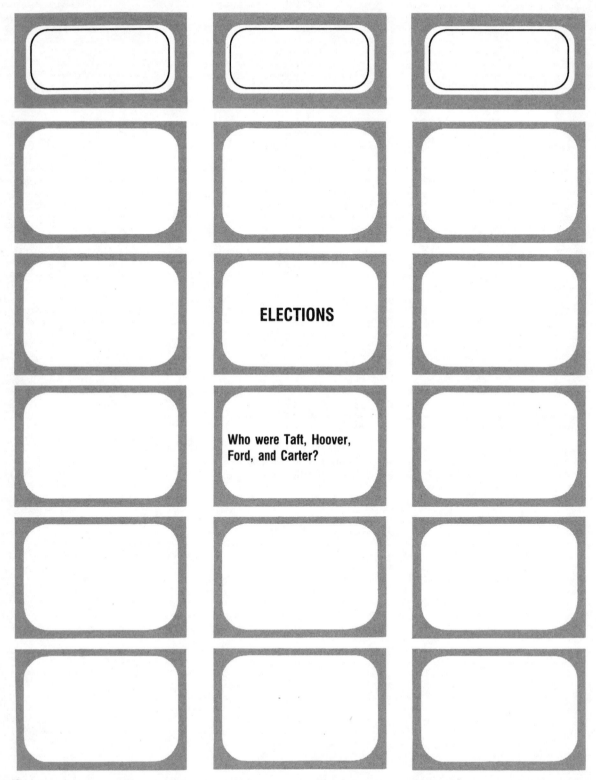

ELECTIONS

Who were Taft, Hoover, Ford, and Carter?

Tournament of Champions #5

JEOPARDY!

WORD ORIGINS

The adjective "ruddy" comes from the old English "rudig," meaning this color

It's a French word meaning "Dutch," and in English it usually refers to a sauce

From the Latin for shield, "scutum," it's a shield bearing a coat of arms

An Arabic word for "poor" gave us this term for a Muslim or Hindu beggar said to have mystical powers

Named for a town in France, this sheer net fabric is used to make bridal veils and tutus

SINGERS

Country singer Lacy J. Dalton was vice president of the ACM, which is this

Some stores refused to stock his *Lovesexy* album because he was nude on the cover

He made his first tour of the U.S. as a solo performer in 1988, and wham!, he was a smash

The 1968 song about "Sittin' on the Dock of the Bay" was a posthumous number-one hit for him

Once Mrs. Andrew Lloyd Webber, she starred on Broadway in *Phantom of the Opera*

PHYSICAL SCIENCE

An American, Theodore Maiman, built the first of these light-amplifying devices in 1960

When burning, sulfur becomes this compound that's used to keep dried fruit from turning brown

It's defined as a form of an element with the same atomic number but different atomic weight

Named for an English scientist, it's a division of classical physics

This era, the age of mammals, represents less than 1 percent of geologic time

AMERICAN LITERATURE	BOTTOMS UP	THE 1980S
An ex-football player who enters the ministry is the subject of this Sinclair Lewis novel	Legend says bats lived in a shed at its rum distillery and one of them is still on its labels	Business is no longer "hopping" in these clubs, now that the last one in the U.S., in Lansing, Michigan, has closed
James M. Cain's first novel, think letters and bells for a clue to its title	Almond-flavored liqueur whose name comes from the Italian for "bitter," not the Italian for "love"	*Forbes* magazine said this singer has overtaken Bill Cosby as the highest-paid entertainer in the world
J. P. Marquand, who won a Pulitzer for *The Late George Apley,* created this Japanese spy/detective	The recipe for Tia Maria came from this island and "has been closely guarded for generations"	This former U.N. Secretary General negotiated a cease-fire between Iraq and Iran
Among his many books for boys are the Ragged Dick and Tattered Tom series	This hazelnut liqueur was named for the mysterious monk who made it 300 years ago	Canada's maple sugar industry is directly endangered by this pollution
Richard Henry Dana's 1840 classic based on a voyage he took around Cape Horn	Called "The world's oldest whiskey distillery," it's in County Antrim, Ireland	A sharp decline in Cabbage Patch doll sales contributed to this toy company's filing Chapter 11

JEOPARDY!

WORD ORIGINS	SINGERS	PHYSICAL SCIENCE
What is red?	What is the Academy of Country Music?	What is a laser?
What is hollandaise?	Who is Prince?	What is sulfur dioxide?
What is an escutcheon?	Who is George Michael?	What is an isotope?
What is a fakir?	Who was Otis Redding?	What is Newtonian physics?
What is tulle?	Who is Sarah Brightman?	What is the Cenozoic Era?

AMERICAN LITERATURE	BOTTOMS UP	THE 1980S
What is *Elmer Gantry?*	What is Bacardi?	What are Playboy clubs?
What is *The Postman Always Rings Twice?*	What is Amaretto?	Who is Michael Jackson?
Who is Mr. Moto?	What is Jamaica?	Who is Javier Pérez de Cuellar?
Who was Horatio Alger (Jr.)?	What is Frangelico?	What is acid rain?
What is *Two Years Before the Mast?*	What is Bushmills?	What is Coleco?

DOUBLE JEOPARDY!

WORLD HISTORY

According to legend, he was a swineherd before he conquered the Incas

As a result of the Napoleonic Wars, this country lost Norway to Sweden in 1814

"Great" King of Prussia whose last words were "I am tired of ruling over slaves"

He had a wife named Cleopatra, a daughter named Cleopatra, and a famous son, Alexander the Great

The Cuban missile crisis made this the tensest month of 1962

THEATER

In the female version of this Neil Simon play, the title characters are named Olive and Florence

The Fantasticks opens with El Gallo singing this song

In this play, Audrey II is described as "a cross between a Venus fly trap and an avocado"

She adapted the stage version of *The Member of the Wedding* from her own novel

His 1956 play *Look Back in Anger* was called "A landmark in the history of the theatre"

LAKES & RIVERS

The longest river in Europe, it's noted for its boatmen

River that runs from Pittsburgh to Cairo—Illinois that is

The German-speaking Swiss call it the Genfersee

Shreveport, Louisiana, and Hanoi, Vietnam, are both on rivers that have this colorful name

Over 300 rivers flow into this largest freshwater lake in Asia, and only one flows out, the Angara

PRESIDENTIAL HOMES	MUSICAL EUROPE	"AND" SO IT GOES
Rancho del Cielo	Some evidence indicates Beethoven moved 79 times during his 35-year stay in this central European capital	In the Pledge of Allegiance, these four words follow "with liberty"
La Casa Pacifica	"Troldhaugen" is the name of the house this Norwegian built a few miles outside Bergen	On a TV variety show, Jackie Gleason's exit line
The Hermitage	On a 1969 album cover, the Beatles are shown crossing this road outside the recording studio	Title of 1956 French film and its 1988 American remake, both directed by Roger Vadim
The Elms	For 10 years, his widow, Constanze, lived in Copenhagen with her second husband, Georg Nissen	Monty Python's Flying Circus borrowed this catch phrase from BBC announcers
Hickory Hill, which he later sold to his brother	You'd have to go to this country to visit museums honoring composer Bedřich Smetana	Pepys often ended his diary entries with these four words referring to the end of the day's affairs

DOUBLE JEOPARDY!

WORLD HISTORY	THEATER	LAKES & RIVERS
Who was Francisco Pizarro?	What is *The Odd Couple?*	What is the Volga?
What is Denmark?	What is "Try to Remember"?	What is the Ohio?
Who was Frederick the Great? (ACC: Frederick II)	What is *Little Shop of Horrors?*	What is Lake Geneva?
Who was Philip of Macedon? (ACC: Philip II)	Who was Carson McCullers?	What is the Red River?
What was October?	Who is John Osborne?	What is Lake Baikal?

PRESIDENTIAL HOMES	MUSICAL EUROPE	"AND" SO IT GOES
Who is Ronald Reagan?	What is Vienna?	What are "and justice for all"?
Who is Richard Nixon?	Who was Edvard Grieg?	What is "And away we go"?
Who was Andrew Jackson?	What is Abbey Road?	What is *And God Created Woman?*
Who was Lyndon B. Johnson?	Who was W. A. Mozart?	What is "And now for something completely different"?
Who was John F. Kennedy?	What is Czechoslovakia?	What is "And so to bed"?

FINAL JEOPARDY!

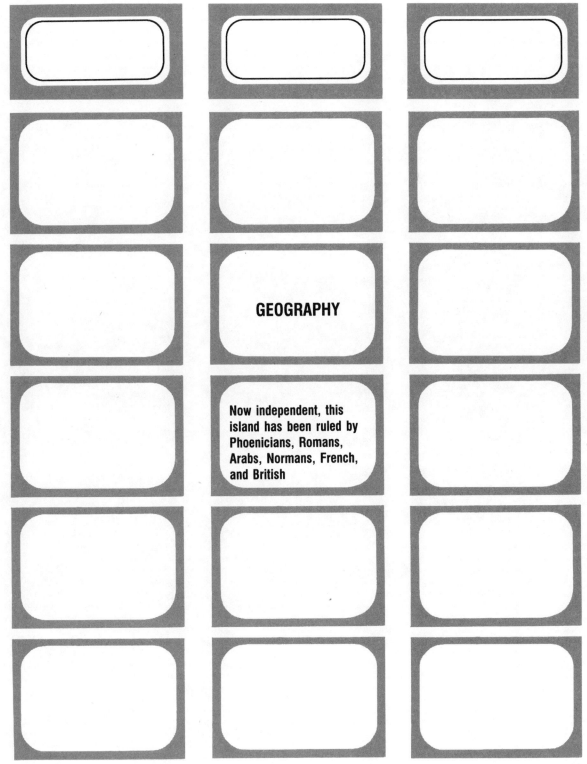

GEOGRAPHY

Now independent, this island has been ruled by Phoenicians, Romans, Arabs, Normans, French, and British

59

FINAL JEOPARDY!

GEOGRAPHY

What is Malta?

Tournament of Champions #6

JEOPARDY!

PLAYS

First performed in the 1550s, *Ralph Roister Doister* is the first known comedy in this language

Little Johnny Jones was the first play he wrote expressly for Broadway, not for vaudeville

Chekhov play that opens with Andrei Prozorov's siblings talking about going to Moscow

Richard Chamberlain and Mary Tyler Moore starred in a 1966 musical flop based on this Truman Capote story

He was almost 90 when he wrote one of his greatest plays, *Oedipus at Colonus*

AVIATION

San Diego, where the plane "Spirit of St. Louis" was built, named its airport for this man

Not surprisingly, in 1939 this nation had the strongest air force in Europe

By definition, a "VTOL" plane can take off and land in this direction

A plane's wings are necessary to create this primary force in flying

In 1909 Louis Blériot electrified the world by flying the 23½ miles of this body of water in 37 minutes

FOOD

Different types of this in the supermarket are labeled "all purpose" and "self-rising"

Called an artichoke, its name isn't from a Mideast city but from "girasole," Italian for sunflower

Add blood, cornstarch, or arrowroot, or try reduction

Shepherd's pie is a meat hash covered with a layer of this

Government graded AA, A, B, or C, the best is composed of at least 80 percent fat and has 12–16 percent water

HOLIDAYS & OBSERVANCES	PIRATES	JOLLY "ROGER"S
If Sugar Ray Leonard is in England on December 26, he might join in the observance of this	In 67 B.C. Pompey's Roman forces cleared out the pirates from this large sea	Maroon Studios star who enjoyed a Diet Coke while watching his wife, Jessica, perform
A Miss, hoping to be a Mrs., might want to observe this November holiday created by Al Capp	"Recruitment" procedure of kidnapping men to work on pirate ships, it's named after a Far Eastern port	This Aussie actor played Aussie police commissioner Robert Scorpio on "General Hospital"
During the Fiesta de San Fermin, these animals run through the streets	Term for a pirate, like Drake, licensed by the crown to capture enemy ships and cargoes	In one episode, she coached Rob's brother, Stacey Petrie, through a practice date
To commemorate this event, some New Englanders celebrate Forefathers' Day on December 21	Sent to Madagascar in the 1690s to battle pirates, this captain allegedly became one himself	As Harcourt Fenton Mudd, he gave Captain Kirk no end of trouble
Military bases are often open to the public on Armed Forces Day, the third Saturday of this month	One of the two well-known women pirates tried and convicted in Jamaica in 1720	Both Elliott Gould and this man played Trapper John McIntyre in "M*A*S*H"

JEOPARDY!

PLAYS	AVIATION	FOOD
What is English?	Who was Charles A. Lindbergh?	What is flour?
Who was George M. Cohan?	What is Germany?	What is Jerusalem artichoke?
What is *Three Sisters?* (ACC: *The Three Sisters*)	What is vertically?	How do you thicken a sauce?
What is "Breakfast at Tiffany's"?	What is lift?	What are mashed potatoes?
Who was Sophocles?	What is the English Channel?	What is butter?

HOLIDAYS & OBSERVANCES

What is Boxing Day?
(ACC: St. Stephen's Day)

What is Sadie Hawkins Day?

What are bulls?

What is the landing of the Mayflower (in 1620)?

What is May?

PIRATES

What is the Mediterranean?

What is Shanghaiing?

What is a privateer?
(ACC: sea dog)

Who was Captain William Kidd?

Who was Anne Bonney or Mary Read?

JOLLY "ROGER"S

Who is Roger Rabbit?

Who is Tristan Rogers?

Who is Sally Rogers?

Who was Roger C. Carmel?

Who is Wayne Rogers?

DOUBLE JEOPARDY!

"C" IN GEOGRAPHY	AUTHORS	THE CABINET

"C" IN GEOGRAPHY

Perry, the barber turned singer, might enjoy visiting this lake and province in Lombardy

AUTHORS

The success of his first novel, *This Side of Paradise,* allowed him to marry Zelda

THE CABINET

The Bureau of Engraving and Printing is part of this department

---

This port city on the east coast of New Zealand's South Island was founded by Anglicans

Born in India, this English author was the youngest person to win a Nobel prize in literature

In 1961 JFK invited our ambassador to this to attend the cabinet meetings

---

Ancient village in Mexico known for the temples and pyramids the Mayans made of brick and stone

Creator of archy and mehitabel, this humorist once was assistant editor for *The Uncle Remus Magazine*

In the 1970s and 1980s he was in charge of first the welfare and later the warfare departments

---

Called France's most famous cheese, it's named for this Normandy village where it was first made

Outsold only by the Bible and Shakespeare, this woman is the best-selling romance writer of the twentieth century

Interior Secretary Harold Ickes was the only cabinet member to serve the full duration of his presidency

---

This capital of Canada's Prince Edward Island was named for the wife of King George III

Author of *Fathers and Sons,* he was the first Russian to be widely read and admired in Europe

In 1973 Henry Kissinger became Nixon's second secretary of state, replacing this man

CLASSICAL MUSIC

Mendelssohn was one of the first to use this to conduct

In a pipe organ, a pipe's shape affects its tone quality, and its length determines this

Of the three "B"s, the one who left town when rejected as Philharmonic conductor in his native Hamburg

Perhaps the greatest violinist ever, this Italian could play a whole piece on just one string

This great concert pianist and Polish premier was a friend of Liberace's family

HISTORY

He became King of Jordan after his mentally ill father was deposed in 1952

The only first lady it ever had was a Mississippi aristocrat named Varina

This lawyer became the leader of the Indian National Congress in 1920

Sir Humphrey Gilbert, half brother of this Elizabethan courtier, drowned while trying to colonize America

An eighteenth-century war was named for this part of Robert Jenkins' body, reputedly cut off by Spaniards

FAMOUS WOMEN

Dame who played Mme. Arcati in *Blithe Spirit* and Miss Marple in the film *Murder She Said*

In 1955 this miniskirt innovator opened her first shop on King's Road in Chelsea

In 1755 Maria Theresa, Queen of Hungary and Bohemia, gave birth to this future queen

The first woman Democrat elected a senator in her own right is this Maryland senator

Patron saint of South America, she was the first canonized saint from the Western hemisphere

DOUBLE JEOPARDY!

"C" IN GEOGRAPHY	AUTHORS	THE CABINET
What is Como?	Who was F. Scott Fitzgerald?	What is the Treasury Department?
What is Christchurch?	Who was Rudyard Kipling?	What is the United Nations?
What is Chichén Itzá?	Who was Don Marquis? (ACC: Donald Robert Perry Marquis)	Who is Casper Weinberger?
What is Camembert?	Who is Barbara Cartland?	Who was FDR?
What is Charlottetown?	Who was Ivan Turgenev?	Who was William P. Rogers?

CLASSICAL MUSIC	HISTORY	FAMOUS WOMEN
What is a baton?	Who is Hussein (I)?	Who is Margaret Rutherford?
What is pitch?	What was the Confederacy? (ACC: Confederate States of America)	Who was Mary Quant?
Who was Johannes Brahms?	Who was (Mahatma) Gandhi? (ACC: Mohandas K. Gandhi)	Who was Marie Antoinette?
Who was Niccolò Paganini?	Who was Sir Walter Raleigh?	Who is Barbara Mikulski?
Who was Ignace Jan Paderewski?	What was his ear?	Who was St. Rose of Lima?

FINAL JEOPARDY!

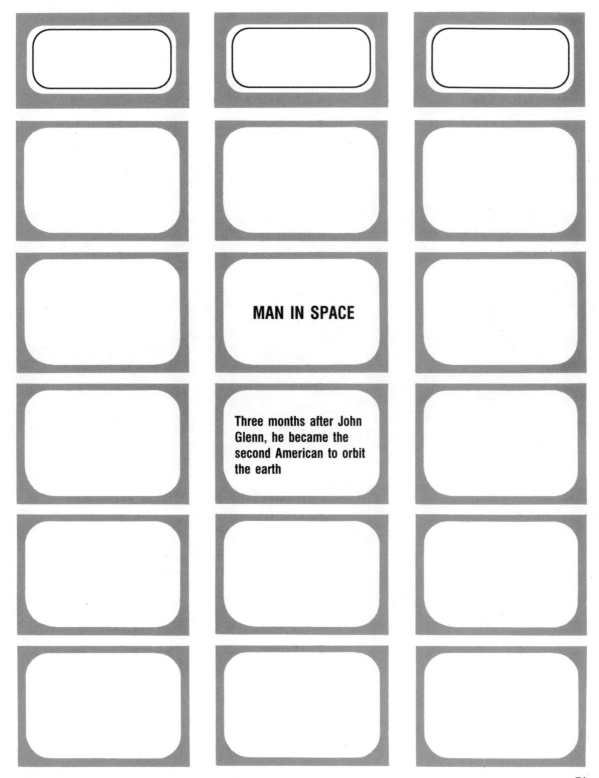

MAN IN SPACE

Three months after John Glenn, he became the second American to orbit the earth

FINAL JEOPARDY!

MAN IN SPACE

Who is (Malcolm) Scott Carpenter?

Tournament of Champions #7

JEOPARDY!

REVOLUTIONS

After the American Revolution, Tom Paine and Lafayette both took part in this revolution

It changed the Western world from a basically rural society to a primarily urban one

This country's revolution had two parts, the February revolution and the October revolution

Using new strains of corn, rice, and wheat, it's the effort to increase food production in the Third World

One-word adjective most commonly used to describe England's bloodless revolution of 1688

INSECTS

To frighten predators, the owl butterfly has large spots on its wings that resemble these

When filled with these, the queen termite can be over four inches long

The plasmodia aren't space invaders but parasites that mosquitos pass to man causing this disease

For sundews and pitcher plants, insects serve this purpose

This type of wasp gets its name from the abnormal protruding plant growths it causes

SILENT MOVIES

The film could have been called "Little Lady Fauntleroy" since it starred her, "America's sweetheart"

This cowboy star's middle initial stood for Surrey

This 1903 Edwin S. Porter classic wasn't filmed in the Wild West but in the wilds of New Jersey

He was White Arm Joe in *The Birth of a Nation,* but is better known as the screen's first Tarzan

In 1914 this actress silently suffered *The Perils of Pauline*

HERBS & SPICES

Related to the banana, it's the spice featured in Vernor's soda

One type of dish in which fenugreek seed is used is this relish from India

Kümmel is one of these flavored with caraway seeds

You can call it laurel leaf or you can call it this, same thing

This herb comes in summer and winter varieties, and its name also means appetizing

SHORT STORIES

"Uncle Wiggily in Connecticut" was one of the *Nine Stories* he published after *The Catcher in the Rye*

Hemingway story in which an African mountain comes to represent purity and escape

Faulkner wrote short and long versions of this story about hunting an enormous animal called "Old Ben"

In this O. Henry story, the kidnappers pay the father $250 to take the kid back

Twain wrote of a stranger who brought a mysterious sack to this town in order to corrupt it—and succeeded

"LONG" SONGS

Phil Spector overdubbed this last number-one Beatles hit; John and Paul's original version is not for sale

First line of the song about an Irish county that's home to "The sweetest girl I know"

Title line that follows "Just kiss me once, then kiss me twice, then kiss me once again"

In *Oliver!*, Nancy, who's in love with Bill Sikes, sings this song of devotion

A 1979 hit by Supertramp gave you these directions for finding your way to your abode

JEOPARDY!

REVOLUTIONS	INSECTS	SILENT MOVIES
What was the French Revolution?	What are eyes?	Who was Mary Pickford?
What was the Industrial Revolution?	What are eggs?	Who was William S. Hart?
What is Russia?	What is malaria?	What is *The Great Train Robbery?*
What is the Green Revolution?	What is a source of food?	Who was Elmo Lincoln?
What is Glorious?	What is the gall wasp?	Who was Pearl White?

HERBS & SPICES

What is ginger?

What is chutney?

What is a liqueur?

What is bay leaf?

What is savory?

SHORT STORIES

Who is J. D. Salinger?

What is "The Snows of Kilimanjaro"?

What is "The Bear"?

What is "The Ransom of Red Chief"?

What is Hadleyburg?

"LONG" SONGS

What is "The Long and Winding Road"?

What is "It's a long way to Tipperary"?

What is "It's Been a Long, Long Time"?

What is "As Long as He Needs Me"?

What is "Take the Long Way Home"?

DOUBLE JEOPARDY!

20TH-CENTURY PERSONALITIES

Born in Russian Poland in 1886, he became the first prime minister of Israel

Use of the term "psyche" for the whole personality was begun by this great Swiss psychiatrist

Jackie Kennedy authorized him to write *The Death of a President,* but later sued to stop publication

Sun Yat-sen was trained as and practiced this profession before entering politics

Like Churchill, this British prime minister, chosen in 1957, had an American mother

TRANSPORTATION

Non-flyer John Madden travels on this, the "Maddencruiser," complete with bed and shower

Doing this comes from the Roman custom of offering a drink to the gods when launching a ship

In addition to a rudder and oars, most keelboats were equipped with these to aid travel

Until 1937 the Lakehurst, New Jersey, naval air station was the U.S. transatlantic terminal for these craft

Bells were rung across the U.S. as telegraphers relayed news of this event on May 10, 1869

DANCERS

She joined the Ballets Russes at 14 and was still a teenager when she married her ballet teacher, Nico Charisse

This tiny star of *Good News* learned to dance by watching a Fred Astaire movie 17 times

This ballerina was born on an Indian reservation in Fairfax, Oklahoma, in 1925

She was a modern dancer in New York long before playing Cinnamon on "Mission: Impossible"

This ballerina wrote a biography of George Balanchine after taking off her "red shoes"

SHAKESPEARE	ISLANDS	X, Y, Z

Canada's best-known theatrical event is the annual festival here featuring plays by Shakespeare

Some call it the island continent

The name of this lakeside Swiss city is believed to be from the Celtic word for "water"

The ghost of his wife, Anne, haunted him at Bosworth Field

A roofed Hawaiian porch, or the Hawaiian island called "The Pineapple Island"

Sergeant Preston's beat

Not only was this king slain by Macbeth, but rumors said his horses ate each other

This island, called "The Rock," had the first lighthouse on the West Coast

Though Dobie Gillis didn't particularly care for it, she kept calling him "Poopsie"

Rejected lover whose last words are "If thou be merciful, open the tomb, lay me with Juliet"

There are islands with this name in Massachusetts, Washington state, Wisconsin, and Maine, but the biggest is in New York

This Michigan city was settled in 1825 and named for a nineteenth-century Greek patriot

---

The title character of this tragedy is governor of Cyprus, where much of the play is set

Island group owned partly by Britain and partly by the U.S.

After his forces were defeated by the Greeks, this Persian king was murdered by his own nobles

DOUBLE JEOPARDY!

20TH-CENTURY PERSONALITIES	TRANSPORTATION	DANCERS
Who was David Ben-Gurion?	What is a (Greyhound) bus?	Who is Cyd Charisse? (ACC: Tula Finklea)
Who was Carl Jung?	What is breaking champagne on the prow? (ACC: Christening a ship)	Who is June Allyson?
Who is William Manchester?	What are sails?	Who is Maria Tallchief?
What is a physician? (ACC: doctor)	What are dirigibles?	Who is Barbara Bain?
Who was Harold Macmillan?	What is completion of the transcontinental railroad?	Who is Moira Shearer?

SHAKESPEARE	ISLANDS	X, Y, Z
What is Stratford, Ontario?	What is Australia?	What is Zurich?
Who is Richard III?	What is Lanai?	What is the Yukon?
Who was (King) Duncan (of Scotland)?	What is Alcatraz?	Who was Zelda (Gilroy)?
Who is Paris?	What is Long Island?	What is Ypsilanti?
What is *Othello?*	What are the Virgin Islands?	Who was Xerxes (I) (the Great)?

FINAL JEOPARDY!

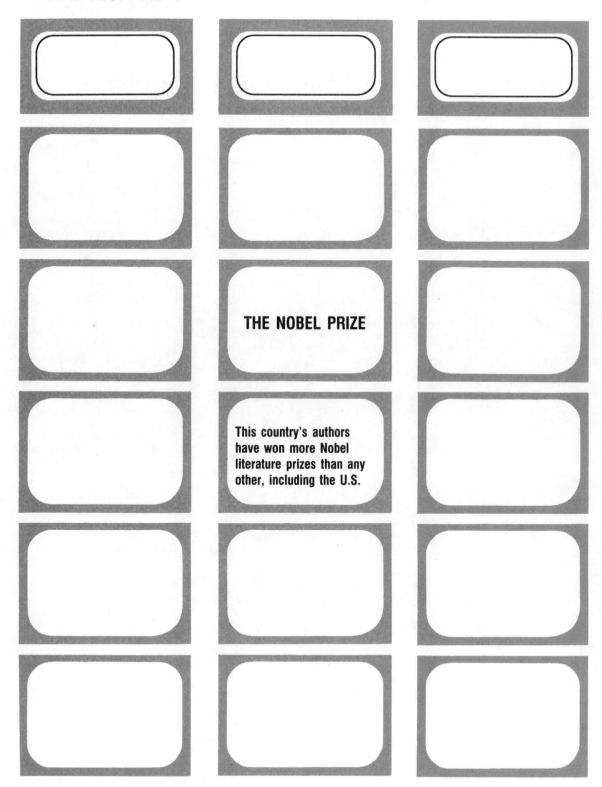

THE NOBEL PRIZE

This country's authors have won more Nobel literature prizes than any other, including the U.S.

THE NOBEL PRIZE

What is France?

Tournament of Champions #8

JEOPARDY!

MOVIES

This *Road Warrior* became a *Lethal Weapon* in 1987

In *20,000 Leagues Under the Sea*, James Mason played this slightly screwy sub skipper

Richard Burton had a devil of a time directing himself in the film version of this Marlowe tragedy

As TV reporter Kimberly Wells, she gave glowing reports in *The China Syndrome*

In *Father Goose*, he played a beachcomber who secretly spotted enemy planes during WWII

BRITISH ROYALTY

One historian claimed this queen secretly married one of her servants after Albert died

She wore a Norman Hartnell gown inspired by a Botticelli painting when she married a lieutenant in 1947

The estate outside Paris where he lived with his duchess is now a private museum

He's second in line to the British throne after his father, Charles

Henry VIII was her third husband, and she married again after he died

TECHNOLOGY

Term for a moving stairway, it was originally a trademark of the Otis Elevator Co.

At the touch of a button, on July 1, 1939, this Clay Puett invention made its horse-racing debut

A 1947 book trumpeted the fact that this new invention could be used to locate thunderstorms

Charles Goodyear vulcanized rubber, and this Charles used rubber to waterproof cloth

The reason the transistor was invented was to make this piece of equipment work better

WYOMINGITES

Nickname of frontierswoman Martha Jane Cannary, who was born in Missouri, lived in Wyoming, and died in South Dakota

In 1925 Nellie Tayloe Ross became the first woman to hold this office in the U.S.

He spent time in Wyoming, though his most famous novel is *The Virginian*

This Wyoming-born abstract expressionist painted with his canvas on the floor

A Wyoming national forest is named for this mountain man who helped map the Oregon Trail

THE PIANO

The keys at both ends of the standard piano keyboard are this color

Two different TV movies about this pianist and piano collector played on consecutive Sundays in 1988

This 135-year-old company keeps a constant bank of about 600 concert grands around the world

The three main kinds of upright pianos are the studio, the console, and this

The Oscar-winning short *The Music Box* featured this pair moving a piano up a steep hill

IN OTHER WORDS . . .

It's impossible to be victorious at every attempt

Entirely well attired without any destination

Rein in one's palominos

Toss one's loaves onto aquatic environments

Buffoon's Utopia

JEOPARDY!

MOVIES	BRITISH ROYALTY	TECHNOLOGY
Who is Mel Gibson?	Who was Queen Victoria?	What is an escalator?
Who is Captain Nemo?	Who is Elizabeth II?	What is the electric starting gate?
What is *Dr. Faustus?*	Who was Edward VIII? (ACC: Duke of Windsor)	What is radar?
Who is Jane Fonda?	Who is Prince William? (William Arthur Philip Louis)	Who was (Charles) Macintosh?
Who is Cary Grant?	Who was Catherine Parr?	What is a telephone (switcher)?

WYOMINGITES	THE PIANO	IN OTHER WORDS . . .
What is "Calamity Jane"?	What is white? (ACC: ivory)	What is "You can't win 'em all"?
What is governor?	Who was Liberace?	What is "All dressed up and no place (nowhere) to go"?
Who was Owen Wister?	What is Steinway (& Sons)?	What is "Hold your horses"?
Who was Jackson Pollock?	What is a spinet?	What is "Cast your bread upon the waters"?
Who was Jim Bridger?	Who are Laurel and Hardy?	What is "A fool's paradise"?

DOUBLE JEOPARDY!

19TH-CENTURY WOMEN

Catherine Booth designed the bonnet worn by women in this semi-military group founded by her husband

British soldiers wounded in the Crimean War called her the "Lady with the lamp"

This famous nineteenth-century beauty had four husbands, including a bigamist, but she never married Jim Brady

In 1893 this Sunday school teacher was the most notorious woman in Fall River, Massachusetts

This abolitionist was born into slavery in New York, and the first language she spoke was Dutch

COOKING

If a recipe calls for blanching tomatoes, it's so that you can remove this more easily

Be alert when you heat oil for frying, because once it reaches the point when it does this, it decomposes

To make pumpernickel, use the dark flour of this grain

It's the difference between a boiled potato and a parboiled one

An Italian dish of veal shanks cooked with white wine, olive oil, spices, tomatoes, and a few anchovies

ANIMALS

Pet owners often buy their dogs and cats a special collar to protect them from fleas and these arachnids

The World Wildlife Fund is working with the Chinese on a detailed survey of pandas and this, their only food

Some of these birds have bald heads and necks, which prevents feather damage when eating from carcasses

In Canada, the population of these tufted-eared wildcats depends on the population of snowshoe rabbits

Caimans are most closely related to these animals

WORLD CITIES

If you receive a Rhodes scholarship, you'll have to hit the road to this city

It's the most famous industry of the Netherlands town of Edam

Though Amman used to be named this, it wasn't home to a "Jordanian Bandstand" TV show

Considered the home of Japanese drama, especially puppet theater, it's Japan's third largest city

If you take a case to the Swiss supreme court, you have to go to this French-speaking city near Geneva

"A" IN LITERATURE

He's a weak-willed king in the Old Testament or a whaler captain in *Moby Dick*

Poe poem about a maiden who "lived with no other thought than to love and be loved by me"

Set in the forest of Arden, this comedy has more songs than any other Shakespeare play

Robin Hood's hyphenated henchman

Booth Tarkington book that ends as the title character enters the stairway to Frincke's business college

SIGNS & SYMBOLS

The two pieces of silverware on the traditional sign for a restaurant

A road sign showing the back of a car with two wavy lines trailing from it stands for this

In *The Talk Book*, Dr. Gerald Goodman figures 25 percent of all we say is followed by this punctuation mark

In weather forecasts, levels of this invisible, irritating gas are symbolized O_3

In a chemical equation this symbol denotes a substance has escaped as a gas

DOUBLE JEOPARDY!

19TH-CENTURY WOMEN

What is the Salvation Army?

Who was Florence Nightingale?

Who was Lillian Russell?

Who was Lizzie Borden?

Who was Sojourner Truth?

COOKING

What is the skin?

What is when it smokes?

What is rye?

What is the parboiled one is not fully cooked?

What is osso buco?

ANIMALS

What are ticks?

What is bamboo?

What are vultures?

What are lynxes?

What are alligators?

WORLD CITIES	"A" IN LITERATURE	SIGNS & SYMBOLS
What is Oxford?	Who is Ahab?	What are a fork and a knife?
What is cheesemaking?	What is "Annabel Lee"?	What is "slippery when wet"?
What is Philadelphia?	What is *As You Like It?*	What is a question mark?
What is Osaka?	Who is Allan-a-Dale?	What is Ozone?
What is Lausanne?	What is *Alice Adams?*	What is an arrow pointing up?

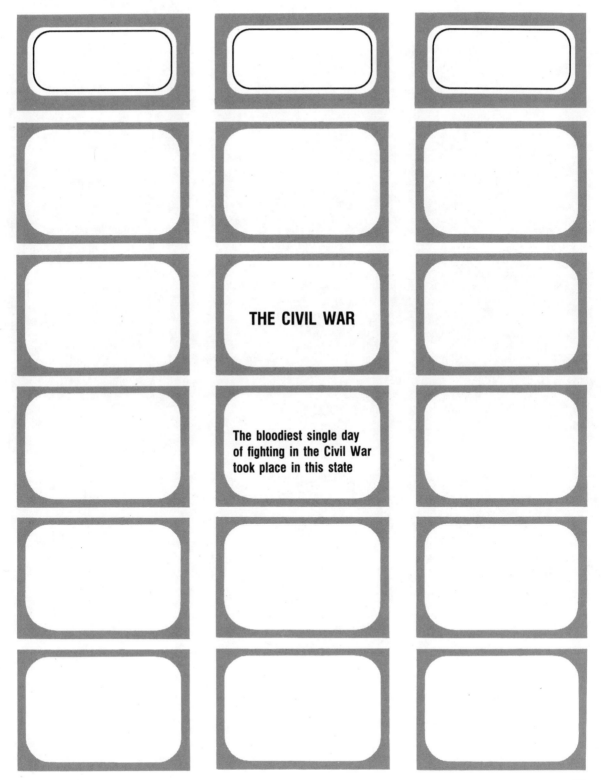

THE CIVIL WAR

The bloodiest single day
of fighting in the Civil War
took place in this state

FINAL JEOPARDY!

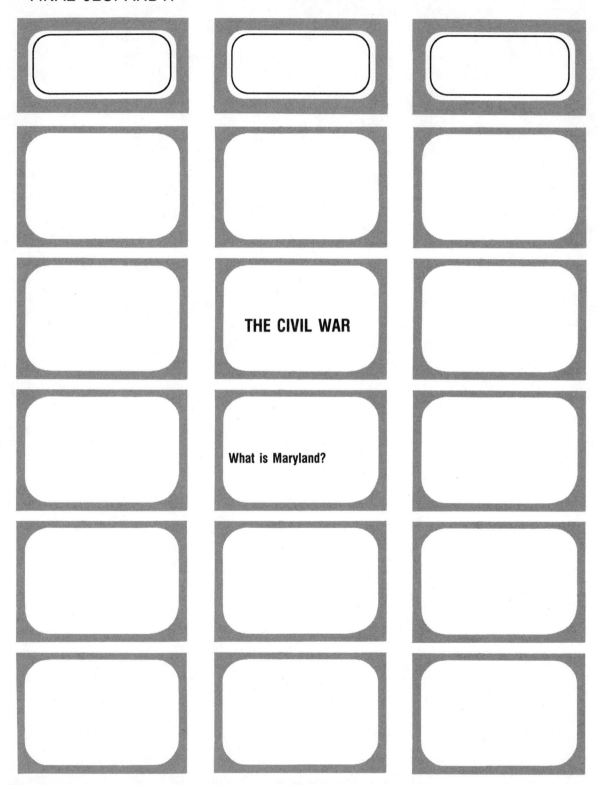

THE CIVIL WAR

What is Maryland?

Tournament of Champions #9

JEOPARDY!

THE 19TH CENTURY

In 1845 and again in 1846 this crop failed in Ireland

Besides farm machines he invented the first practical rapid-fire machine gun in the U.S.

In 1880 this state became the first whose population exceeded 5 million

Austrian archduke who became emperor of Mexico in 1863

In the early nineteenth century they collected tales from the people around Kassel, Germany

CHOREOGRAPHERS

When Balanchine staged *Orpheus and Eurydice* at this U.S. opera house, he kept the singers in the pit

This modern dancer created over 170 works; her career spanned the century

In a single year he choreographed *42nd Street, Footlight Parade,* and *Gold Diggers of 1933*

He conceived, directed, and choreographed *West Side Story*

In the original 1942 production of *Rodeo,* she danced the role of the cowgirl

FAMILIAR PHRASES

Trying to find similarities between New York and L.A. is like comparing these

The biblical phrase "give up the ghost" means this

"He has more money than you can" do this "at"

From the tradition of men fighting topless came this saying urging calm

Originally a caption in silent Westerns, it returned your attention to the main house

98

SEWING

A bodkin is a large blunt one of these used to draw cord or elastic through a casing

Finishing this, which should be invisible, is usually the last step in making a dress

A twill fabric with a zigzag pattern, or what can stick in your throat when you eat a certain fish

These are folds of fabric pressed to resemble the bellows of a squeezebox

It's fabric that gives body and shape to a collar, not two computers talking

ALABAMIANS

William Wyatt Bibb, Thomas Bibb, Bibb Graves, and George Wallace all held this office

He was born Nathaniel Adams Coles but was best known under this "unforgettable" name

Though he was born near Lafayette, Alabama, the arena named after this boxer is in Detroit

Gawl-ee! This man, born in Sylacauga, has had two top-40 albums

In his last major opinion, this "colorful" Supreme Court justice upheld the *New York Times'* right to publish the Pentagon Papers

SILLY SONGS

Song that says, "Roll out the barrel, we'll have a barrel of fun," is named for this type of barrel

Two of the animals you're urged not to be like in "Swinging on a Star"

"It's the only thing that I could do half right, and it's turnin' out all wrong, Ma"

1950s hit that begins, "Life could be a dream, if I could take you up to paradise up above"

Song whose chorus goes, "Valderi valdera valdera valde ha ha ha ha ha ha . . ."

JEOPARDY!

THE 19TH CENTURY

What was the potato crop?

Who was Richard Gatling?

What is New York?

Who was Maximilian?

Who were the Brothers Grimm?

CHOREOGRAPHERS

What is the Met(ropolitan Opera House)?

Who was Martha Graham?

Who was Busby Berkeley?

Who is Jerome Robbins?

Who is Agnes de Mille?

FAMILIAR PHRASES

What are apples and oranges?

What is die?

What is "shake a stick"? (ACC: poke a stick)

What is "Keep your shirt on"?

What is "Meanwhile, back at the ranch"?

SEWING

What is a needle?

What is a hem?
(DNA: seam)

What is (a) herringbone?

What are accordion pleats?

What is interfacing?

ALABAMIANS

Who were governors of Alabama?

Who was Nat King Cole?

Who was Joe Louis?

Who is Jim Nabors?

Who was Hugo Black?

SILLY SONGS

What is a beer barrel?

What is a mule, a pig, a fish, and monkeys?

What is "(What Have They Done to) My Song (Ma)"?

What is "Sh-Boom"?

What is "The Happy Wanderer"?

DOUBLE JEOPARDY!

SHAKESPEAREAN 1ST LINES

This fairy king's first line is "Ill met by moonlight, proud Titania"

Famous "tamer" who enters saying, "Verona, for a while I take my leave"

Warrior who says, "Call here my varlet; I'll unarm again; why should I war without the walls of Troy . . ."

His first line consists of just one word, "Calphurnia!"

King of Denmark who begins, "Though yet of Hamlet our dear brother's death the memory be green . . ."

OLD MOVIES

This classic 1939 John Wayne Western was partly based on the short story "Stage to Lordsburg"

Marlene Dietrich played Shanghai Lily in this 1932 film named for a Chinese train

Jimmy Stewart killed a Mountie in this 1936 musical, so singing Mountie Nelson Eddy chased him

In the last scene of *Casablanca,* Claude Rains tells one of his officers to "Round up" these

Bob Hope sang this Oscar-winning song with Jane Russell in *The Paleface*

ARTISTS

This *Maja* artist said he recognized only three masters: Velázquez, Rembrandt, and nature

In 1922 Marc Chagall left this country, his native land

He painted one of his most famous pictures, *Christina's World,* 40 years ago

This Iowan was a leader of regionalism, a movement that dominated U.S. art in the 1930s

In 1485 this Italian painted *Madonna of the Rocks,* his earliest major work that survives in complete form

THE 50 STATES

All of the present District of Columbia is on land originally donated by this state

As the insurance company commercials remind us, Wausau isn't in Poland but in this state

A city is named for the great falls of the Missouri River in this state

This state's capital lies on Cook Inlet, west of the Chugach Mountains

Elizabeth Garrett, the blind daughter of sheriff Pat Garrett, wrote the state song of this 47th state

TRANSPORTATION

Ironically, this Chicago airport was named for a naval hero

On July 21, 1959, the first cargo ship powered by this was launched at Camden, New Jersey

In 1957 an Air Force doctor stayed a record 32 hours in the stratosphere in one of these

In the Old West, this railroad, named for three cities, was said to have "started nowhere and went nowhere"

With over 200,000 miles of railroad tracks, this country has more than any other

PRESIDENTIAL LAST WORDS

His last words, spoken in Warm Springs, Georgia, were "I have a terrific headache"

"I've always loved my wife, my children and grandchildren, and I've always loved my country," he said in 1969

"Thomas Jefferson survives"

Though noted for his drinking, the last thing he said was "Water"

"I know that I'm going where Lucy is," Lemonade Lucy that is

DOUBLE JEOPARDY!

SHAKESPEAREAN 1ST LINES	OLD MOVIES	ARTISTS
Who is Oberon?	What is *Stagecoach?*	Who was (Francisco) Goya?
Who is Petruchio?	What was *Shanghai Express?*	What is USSR? (ACC: Belorussia)
Who is Troilus?	What was *Rose Marie?*	Who is Andrew Wyeth?
Who is Julius Caesar?	What are "the usual suspects"?	Who was Grant Wood?
Who is (King) Claudius?	What is "Buttons and Bows"?	Who was Da Vinci?

THE 50 STATES	TRANSPORTATION	PRESIDENTIAL LAST WORDS
What is Maryland?	What is O'Hare?	Who was FDR?
What is Wisconsin?	What is nuclear power?	Who was Dwight D. Eisenhower?
What is Montana?	What is a balloon?	Who was John Adams?
What is Alaska?	What was the Atchison, Topeka & Santa Fe?	Who was Ulysses S. Grant?
What is New Mexico?	What is the U.S.?	Who was Rutherford B. Hayes?

THE SUPREME COURT

Only member of the current court who has been elected to a public office

FINAL JEOPARDY!

THE SUPREME COURT

Who is Sandra Day O'Connor?

Tournament of Champions #10

JEOPARDY!

FIRST NAMES

You don't have to know it was Pulitzer's first name to win a Pulitzer prize

The dynamite first name of the founder of the Nobel prizes

Were he alive, you would call him by this first name to thank him for a Rhodes scholarship

Colonel Sanders of "finger lickin'" fame

According to Hoyle, it was his first name

U.S. STATES

The largest U.S. naval base is at Norfolk in this state

The two U.S. states that begin with "N" that are neither "north" nor "new"

Among its 77 counties are Creek, Cherokee, Choctaw, Seminole, and Osage

Its state song is "Home on the Range," not "Over the Rainbow"

Named for John Jacob Astor, Astoria, first American settlement west of the Rockies, is in this state

POETS

Georgia poet Sidney Lanier spent several months in a Maryland prison during this war

In one of his cute couplets he quipped, "A bit of talcum is always walcum"

Ralph Waldo Emerson spent much of his life in this New England state where he was born

This nineteenth-century poet laureate was the most famous poet born in the Lake District of England

This Maine poetess sometimes wrote under the shorter pen name Nancy Boyd

THE BODY HUMAN

These smallest blood-carrying tubes in the body link arteries to veins

To prevent rejection of transplanted organs, doctors suppress these blood cells

Though associated with ill temper, this organ actually produces antibodies

The integumentary system is another term for this, the body's largest organ

The scientific name for the shinbone

1979

Acronym used to refer to the treaty signed by Brezhnev and Carter in Vienna in June

This Boston outfielder became the first American League player to get both 3,000 hits and 400 home runs

It was the no. 2 reactor at this Pennsylvania site that caused fears of a meltdown

Amity Island was the setting for this 1975 film that topped 1979's TV ratings

This general resigned as Supreme Commander of NATO and also retired from the U.S. Army

CELEBRITY RELATIVES

Larry Hagman's mom, who was famous for playing a boy

Dr. Zhivago wasn't this actress' first film; as a child she appeared in her father's film *Limelight*

Mariska Hargitay, who appeared on "Falcon Crest," is the daughter of this late sex symbol

This former brother-in-law of Angela Lansbury co-starred with her in *Death on the Nile* as Hercule Poirot

Singer whose ex-son-in-law, Sidney Lumet, directed her in *The Wiz,* in the role of a witch

JEOPARDY!

FIRST NAMES	U.S. STATES	POETS
What is Joseph?	What is Virginia?	What was the Civil War?
What is Alfred?	What are Nevada and Nebraska?	Who is Ogden Nash?
What is Cecil?	What is Oklahoma?	What was Massachusetts?
What is Harland?	What is Kansas?	Who was William Wordsworth?
What is Edmond?	What is Oregon?	Who was Edna St. Vincent Millay?

THE BODY HUMAN	1979	CELEBRITY RELATIVES
What are capillaries?	What was the Salt (II) Treaty?	Who is Mary Martin?
What are lymphocytes? (ACC: white blood cells)	Who is Carl Yastrzemski?	Who is Geraldine Chaplin?
What is the spleen?	What is Three Mile Island?	Who is Jayne Mansfield?
What is the skin?	What is *Jaws?*	Who is Peter Ustinov?
What is the tibia?	Who is Alexander Haig?	Who is Lena Horne?

DOUBLE JEOPARDY!

ANCIENT TIMES

He built Babylon's Ishtar Gate as well as the Hanging Gardens

The place in Egypt where Jacob settled was known to the Hebrews as the Land o' . . . this

Byzantine emperor who built the Hagia Sophia Church and collected Roman laws into one code

With the defeat of this man at Actium in 31 B.C., Octavian had full control of the Roman Empire

The ancient Persian holy book, called the *Avesta,* contains the writings of this man and his followers

COLLEGES

In the 1940s the University of Chicago came to be recognized as the birthplace of this type of energy

In 1779 this Virginia institution became the first U.S. college to establish a law department

It ends its cheer, "cosine, secant, tangent, sine, 3.14159; integral, radical, u dv; slipstick, slide rule . . ."

This Ivy League school is the land grant college of New York State

The University of Dublin, which has its own representative in the Irish Parliament, is also called this

MUSIC

The written notes for all the instruments and voices of a particular work, or Tigers 5 Yankees 3

A concertino is a short concerto, and a concertina is a simple one of these instruments

Before he composed the *London* Symphony in 1795, he had written the six Paris symphonies

Name shared by the operatic heroines of *Fidelio* and *Il Trovatore*

The famous "Sabre Dance" is from this Soviet-Armenian composer's ballet *Gayane*

MOUNTAINS

Due to the number of climbers, the Park Service may put an outhouse at the 17,000′ level of this Alaskan peak

The third highest peak in North America is in this third largest country in North America

Mountain ranges on this continent include the Queen Elizabeth, Queen Alexandra, and Queen Maud

This Englishman was the first to survey K2's peak

Today climbers can make it from the Chamonix city hall to the top of this mountain and back in less than 5½ hours

NATIONAL LEADERS

President Mitterrand is this country's head of state

Prime Minister Mulroney

President Mubarak

Queen Margrethe II

Prime Minister Mugabe

CHARACTERS IN PLAYS

Shaw character who thinks she's descended from a sacred cat and that her blood is made with Nile water

The first line of this Strindberg play tells us that the title "miss" is "absolutely wild!"

In Euripides' tragedy, Jason's new wife is burned alive by a wedding gift from this woman

Violet Venable's son, who never appears in the play *Suddenly Last Summer* because he's been eaten

At the end of *Who's Afraid of Virginia Woolf?* he realizes that George and Martha's son is imaginary

DOUBLE JEOPARDY!

ANCIENT TIMES

Who was Nebuchadnezzar (II)?

What is Goshen?

Who was Justinian (I)?

Who was Mark Antony? (ACC: Marcus Antonius)

Who was Zoroaster?

COLLEGES

What is nuclear?

What is William and Mary?

What is MIT?

What is Cornell?

What is Trinity College?

MUSIC

What is a score?

What is an accordion?

Who was Franz Joseph Haydn?

What is Leonora?

Who was Aram Khachaturian?

MOUNTAINS	NATIONAL LEADERS	CHARACTERS IN PLAYS
What is Mt. McKinley?	What is France?	Who is Cleopatra?
What is Mexico?	What is Canada?	Who is Miss Julie?
What is Antarctica?	What is Egypt?	Who is Medea?
Who was (Henry Haversham) Godwin-Austen?	What is Denmark?	Who was Sebastian (Venable)?
What is Mt. Blanc?	What is Zimbabwe?	Who is Nick?

FINAL JEOPARDY!

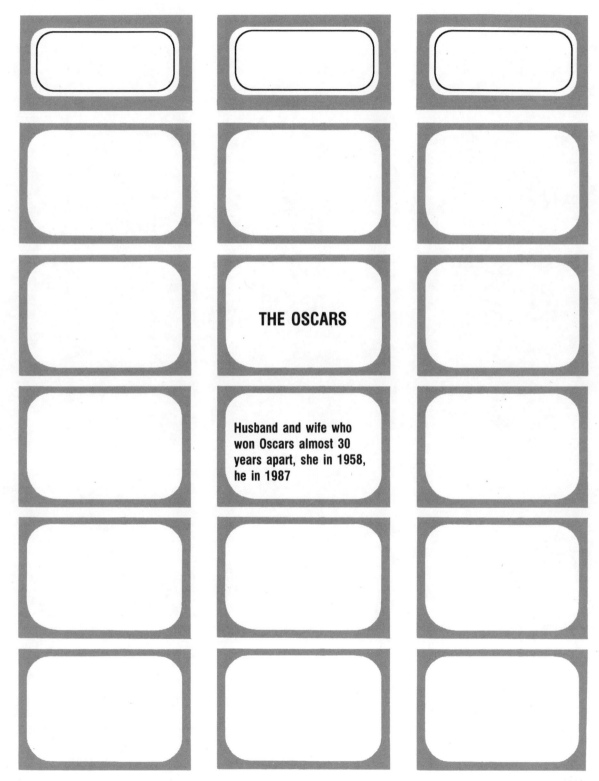

THE OSCARS

Husband and wife who won Oscars almost 30 years apart, she in 1958, he in 1987

FINAL JEOPARDY!

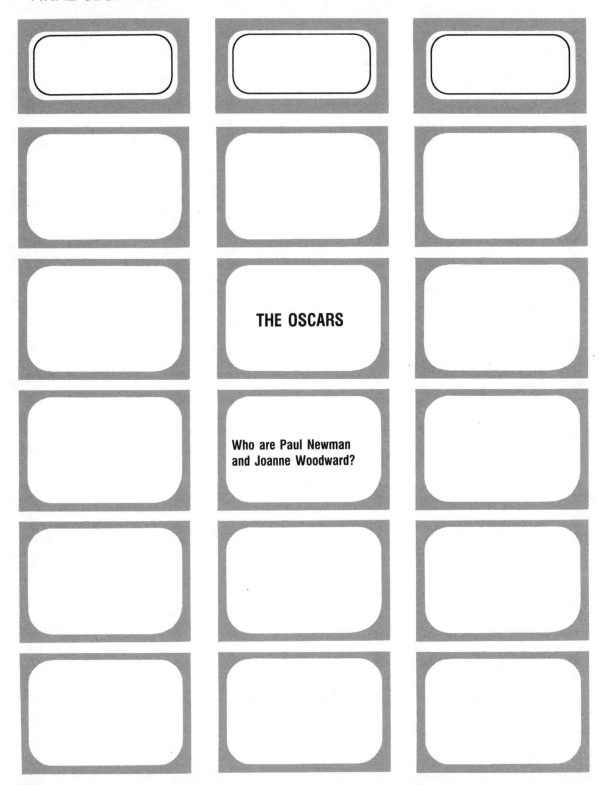

THE OSCARS

Who are Paul Newman and Joanne Woodward?

Tournament of Champions #11

JEOPARDY!

"FOUR" WORDS

50¢

King, king, king, king, or three, three, three, three, for example

An auto worker on the night shift might install this shift

"Sweet Adeline," sung by a barbershop quartet, features a blend of melody lines described as this

A necktie tied a certain way, or a horse-drawn vehicle driven by one person

MOVIE TRIVIA

Woody Allen's first line in this film is "Chapter 1. He adored New York City. He idolized it . . ."

In *The Wizard of Oz,* she was the first character to wear the ruby slippers

The names of these two movie elephants differ by just one letter

Though he was best known for directing musicals, the last film he directed was a drama, *Star 80*

Marlon Brando and his motorcycle pals ganged up on a small town in this 1954 film

POTENT POTABLES

A fifth equals about ⅕ of this

Claiming U.S. creation of this "Gaelic" drink, San Francisco's Buena Vista Café sells some 2,200 cups daily

This strong, dark type of beer takes its name from Einbeck, Germany, where it was first made

It's usually made with bourbon, sugar, mint, and crushed ice

Whiskey sours and daiquiris are similar except that daiquiris contain this instead of whiskey

NAMES IN THE NEWS	THE REVOLUTIONARY WAR	HAIR CARE
After he moved out of his office on Pennsylvania Avenue, he rented an office in Los Angeles	A statue in New York of this leader was toppled and later melted into American bullets	As a dessert, it can add weight to your body; as a styling product, it can add body to your hair
Yuri Churbanov, son-in-law of this former Soviet leader, was tried for taking bribes	Washington attempted to kidnap this man and have him returned to U.S. forces for execution	Style in which hair is rolled under at shoulder length, or a young male attendant at a hotel
This leader of the yippies in the 1960s made his debut as a comedian in a New York club in 1988	The first page of this 1776 pamphlet reads, "Government even in its best state is but a necessary evil."	In dollars, America's biggest-selling shampoo is this one for controlling dandruff
Larry Doyle and Neal Sternecky revived this comic strip that Walt Kelly created	This March 1770 event began with a group of rowdies hurling insults and snowballs at British soldiers	Hair care item that's mentioned in "Bill Bailey"
In September 1988 a storm forced his plane to land at Johannesburg, though it wasn't on his itinerary	This Philadelphia building hosted the first Continental Congress, though delegates didn't carry hammers	He was flown from London to Hollywood just to cut Mia Farrow's hair for the film *Rosemary's Baby*

JEOPARDY!

"FOUR" WORDS	MOVIE TRIVIA	POTENT POTABLES
What is four bits?	What is *Manhattan?*	What is a U.S. gallon?
What is four of a kind?	Who was the Wicked Witch (of the East)?	What is Irish coffee?
What is a four-on-the-floor? (ACC: four-speed)	What are "Jumbo" and "Dumbo"?	What is bock (beer)?
What is four-part (harmony)?	Who was Bob Fosse?	What is a mint julep?
What is a four-in-hand?	What is *The Wild One?*	What is rum?

NAMES IN THE NEWS	THE REVOLUTIONARY WAR	HAIR CARE
Who is Ronald Reagan?	Who was George III?	What is mousse?
Who is (Leonid) Brezhnev?	Who was Benedict Arnold?	What is a page boy?
Who was Abbie Hoffman?	What was *Common Sense?*	What is Head & Shoulders?
What is "Pogo"?	What was the Boston Massacre?	What is a fine-tooth comb?
Who is the Pope? (John Paul II)	What is Carpenter's Hall?	Who is Vidal Sassoon?

DOUBLE JEOPARDY!

AFRICA

If we ever did a "Starts with 'Rw'" category, this is the only country you'd find in it

Ocean on the Ivory Coast's coast

Despite its name, the Equator does not run through this African country

The two African countries that share land borders with Egypt

It has not one, not two, but three capital cities

MISSIONARIES

He was the missionary credited with converting Ireland to Christianity

In the sixth century B.C. he sent monks to spread his teachings throughout India

After the queen of this South Seas island expelled French missionaries, France took over the island

In the 1890s, the Missionary party, led by Sanford Dole, forced this queen to abdicate

Junipero Serra, who founded all those missions in California, was a member of this order

THE STARS

This force is so strong in a black hole that it doesn't even allow light to escape

Every second the sun converts about 4 million tons of this into helium

No kidding, this star has been described as the nose of the constellation Canis Major

Term for a rapidly spinning neutron star that emits radio waves

This closely spaced group of stars is named after a group of seven sisters

CHILDREN'S LITERATURE

In Clement Moore's most famous poem, they "were hung by the chimney with care"

He kept his wife in a pumpkin shell

Ward Greene's story of the same name inspired this 1955 Disney doggie romance

Near the end of *Through the Looking Glass*, this queen disappears in a bowl of soup

This German studied law but was more famous for his *Tales*, which inspired an 1881 Offenbach opera

STATE POSTAL ABBREVIATIONS

Your friendly family physician, or his state postal abbreviation, if he lives in Maryland

This postal abbreviation identifies Idaho

This state's postal abbreviation is alphabetically first

They're the two states whose postal abbreviations end with the letter "C"

It's the only state whose postal abbreviation is a pronoun

HISTORIC WOMEN

In the 1880s Roseanna McCoy added fuel to her family's feud by falling in love with a man named this

Iva Toguri d'Aquino, a California-born UCLA graduate, was known by this nickname during WWII

She became U.S. ambassador to Italy 18 years after marrying the publisher of *Time*

This Roman emperor's third wife, Messalina, was messing around, so he had her killed

This American-born saint was a widow with five children when she converted to Catholicism

DOUBLE JEOPARDY!

AFRICA	MISSIONARIES	THE STARS
What is Rwanda?	Who was St. Patrick?	What is gravity?
What is the Atlantic Ocean?	Who was Buddha? (ACC: Siddhārtha Gautama)	What is hydrogen?
What is Equatorial Guinea?	What is Tahiti?	What is Sirius?
What are Libya and Sudan?	Who was (Queen) Liliuokalani?	What is a pulsar?
What is South Africa?	What are the Franciscans? (ACC: Order of Friars Minor)	What are the Pleiades?

CHILDREN'S LITERATURE	STATE POSTAL ABBREVIATIONS	HISTORIC WOMEN
What were "The stockings"?	What is MD?	What is Hatfield?
Who was Peter, Peter, pumpkin-eater?	What is ID?	What is Tokyo Rose?
What is *Lady and the Tramp?*	What is Alaska (AK)?	Who was Clare Boothe Luce?
Who is the White Queen?	What are North Carolina and South Carolina?	Who was Claudius?
Who was E. T. A. Hoffmann? (ACC: Ernst Theodor Amadeus Hoffmann)	What is Maine (ME)?	Who was Mother Seton? (ACC: Elizabeth Ann Seton)

FINAL JEOPARDY!

FOREIGN PHRASES

The Greek expression meaning "philosophy (is) the guide of life" is abbreviated by these three Greek letters

FINAL JEOPARDY!

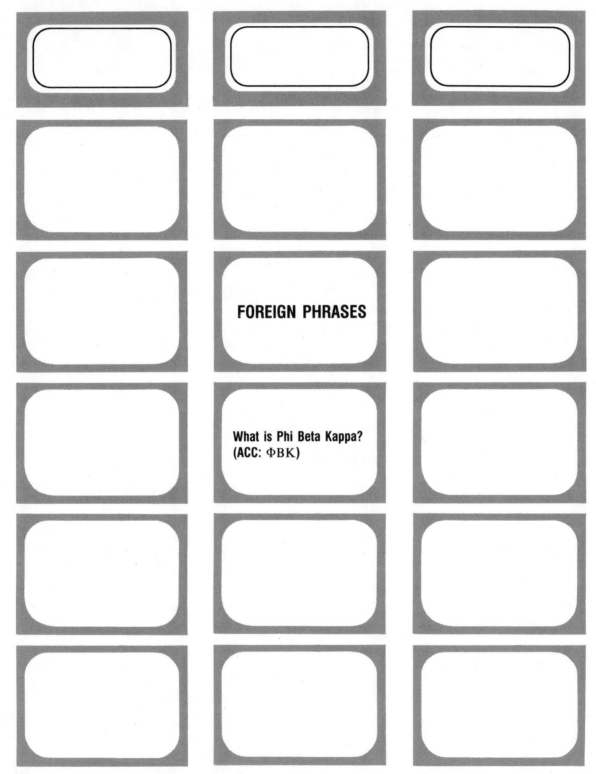

FOREIGN PHRASES

What is Phi Beta Kappa?
(ACC: ΦΒΚ)

Tournaments of Champions #12

JEOPARDY!

WORLD HISTORY

France's 1778 recognition of this nation's independence was a virtual declaration of war on Britain

Frederick II agreed to lead one of these for the Pope, but due to an epidemic he didn't go and was excommunicated

The Congress held here hoped to restore Europe to the way it was before Napoleon

In 1570 Spain's Philip II tried to put this queen on the English throne

This war was thought to be mythical until late nineteenth century excavations proved it really occurred

CARDS & DICE

Number 4 on the dice or the number 3 Cartwright son

Term for the combination of the queen of spades and jack of diamonds in the trick-taking 48-card game

Of the numbers you can throw on your first roll in craps to win, it's the harder to hit

In poker, the number of face cards in a royal flush

The odds of your being dealt this bridge hand are about 635,013,559,599 to 1

U.S. GEOGRAPHY

The lower part of this New York river is an arm of the Atlantic Ocean

Of desert, swamp, or forest, the type of land comprising almost one third of the U.S.

They are South Dakota's example of dome mountains, which are raised up by pressure in the earth's crust

There is a salt lake on this island, Hawaii's third largest

This 107-mile-long lake helps separate New England from New York

LIGHTS	CAMERAS	"ACTION"
The hollowed, carved fruit of the *Cucurbita pepo* plant with a light inside	To frame the subject, one looks through this on most cameras	Slang for a share of the profits
It's a very slender candle or the wax-coated wick used to light it	A new video camera shoots in this process that requires special glasses to view	A departing game-show contestant might receive one of these chairs by Lane
Color of the bulb in all theatrical spotlights	The twin-lens reflex camera under this brand name was introduced in 1928	Movies about Detroit policemen included *Robocop* and this film starring Carl Weathers
Fairy tale that includes the line "Who will change old lamps for new?"	This company made the Fun Touch, One Touch, Action Touch, and Tele-Touch cameras	A rocket lifting off is an example of the third law of motion, which states this
Originally an explosion of gunpowder in a flintlock rifle that failed to set off the charge	Many consider this, whose name is New Latin for "dark chamber," the earliest form of the camera	In 1965 Freddy Cannon intoned, "Oh baby come on let me take you" there

135

JEOPARDY!

WORLD HISTORY	CARDS & DICE	U.S. GEOGRAPHY
What is the U.S.?	What is Little Joe?	What is the Hudson River?
What is a Crusade?	What is Pinochle?	What is forest land?
What is Vienna?	What is 11?	What are the Black Hills?
Who was Mary Stuart (or Mary Queen of Scots)?	What is three?	What is Oahu?
What was the Trojan War?	What is a full suit of 13 cards? (ACC: any specific set of 13 cards)	What is Lake Champlain?

LIGHTS	CAMERAS	"ACTION"
What is a jack-o'-lantern? (ACC: pumpkin)	What is the (view) finder?	What is "a piece of the action"?
What is a taper?	What is 3-D?	What is an action recliner?
What is white?	What is Rolleiflex?	What is *Action Jackson*?
What is "(The History of) Aladdin"?	What is Nikon?	What is "For each action there is an equal and opposite reaction"?
What is a flash in the pan?	What is the camera obscura?	What is "Where the action is"?

DOUBLE JEOPARDY!

WOMEN

A recent survey indicated the status of women in this Scandinavian country is the highest in the world

In 1947 she became the first woman from the U.S. to win the British Women's Amateur Golf Tournament

A former researcher for New York's Mayor Lindsay, she is now a correspondent on "60 Minutes"

The only two women ever to give Democratic Convention keynote speeches were these Texans

Barbara Gordon's book that deals with relationships involving younger women and older men

MYTHS & LEGENDS

Both the Greek and Egyptian Sphinxes had the body of this animal

The Norse hero Sigurd the Dragon Slayer was known to the Germans by this name

Maui taught the Hawaiians to use fire but didn't get in trouble for it like this Greek Titan did

Sir James George Frazer's 12-volume study of ancient myths, its title refers to a mythical branch

This guy's epic was found preserved on 12 tablets in the ruins of Nineveh

SICKNESS & HEALTH

Dr. Spock says this common form of infant dermatitis "is mostly caused by ammonia"

It's the term for any substance that causes an allergic reaction

It's the removal of a piece of tissue from a living body usually for diagnostic study

Plantar warts are found only on this part of the body

There had been epidemics of this lung disease before it was first identified in 1976 in Pennsylvania

POETRY

Edgar Guest said, "It takes a heap o' livin' in a house t' make it" this

English poet who wrote, "She walks in beauty, like the night of cloudless climes and starry skies"

"Water, water everywhere, nor any drop to drink" immortalized this ocean's briny brew

In "Ode on a Grecian Urn" he asked, "What men or gods are these?"

In "On his Blindness" this blind poet wrote, "They also serve who only stand and wait"

COLORFUL PHRASES

In 1965 Vic Dana, Bert Kaempfert, and Wayne Newton all suggested red roses for her

An official statement of government policy, or an NBC news special

Flowers from a citrus tree traditionally used in bridal bouquets

Ornate, flowery writing characterized by an excess of sentiment or pathos

In *Ivanhoe,* when King Richard was in disguise he was described as this

1930S TV

The first known TV adaptation of a story about this detective was 1937's "The Three Garridebs"

In 1937 it broadcast a coronation procession—live!

In a 1939 production, Dennis Hoey played Rochester and Flora Campbell this Brontë heroine

Later starring as "Beulah," this singer known for "Stormy Weather" appeared on a 1939 NBC variety show

FDR was televised at the ceremonies opening this in April 1939

DOUBLE JEOPARDY!

WOMEN	MYTHS & LEGENDS	SICKNESS & HEALTH
What is Sweden?	What is a lion?	What is diaper rash?
Who was Babe Didrikson?	Who is Siegfried?	What is an allergen?
Who is Lesley Stahl?	Who was Prometheus?	What is a biopsy?
Who are Barbara Jordan (1976) and Ann Richards (1988)?	What is *The Golden Bough?*	Where are the feet?
What is *Jennifer Fever?*	Who was Gilgamesh?	What is Legionnaire's Disease?

POETRY	COLORFUL PHRASES	1930S TV
What is (a) home?	Who is a blue lady?	Who is Sherlock Holmes?
Who was Lord Byron?	What is a white paper?	What is the BBC?
What is the Pacific?	What are orange blossoms?	Who is Jane Eyre?
Who was John Keats?	What is purple prose?	Who was Ethel Waters?
Who was John Milton?	What is the Black Knight?	What was the New York World's Fair?

FINAL JEOPARDY!

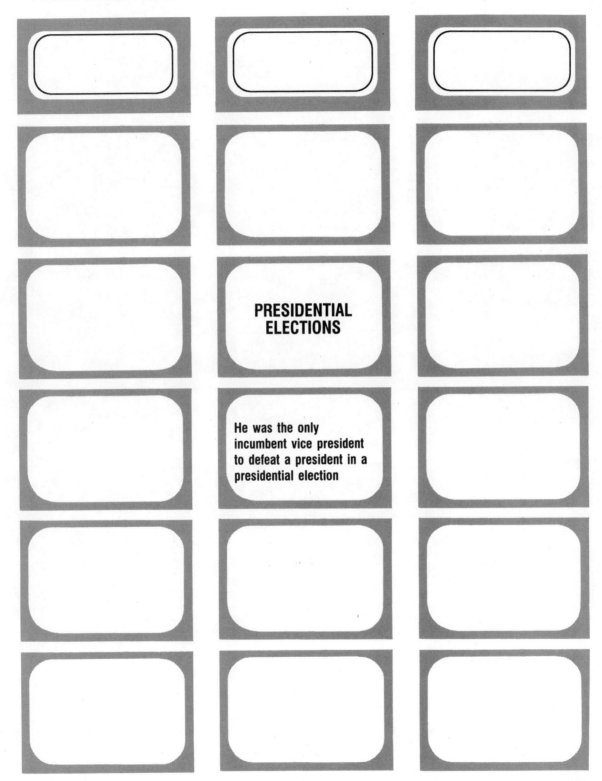

PRESIDENTIAL ELECTIONS

He was the only incumbent vice president to defeat a president in a presidential election

FINAL JEOPARDY!

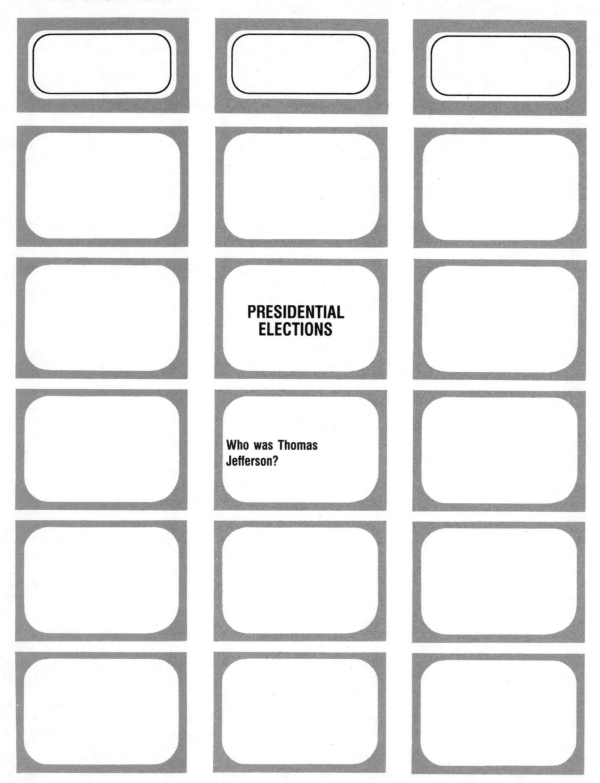

PRESIDENTIAL
ELECTIONS

Who was Thomas
Jefferson?

Tournament of Champions #13

JEOPARDY!

PRESIDENTS

The only president who died in the eighteenth century

One of the two presidents' widows who remarried

The first time this group played for an inauguration was at James Monroe's in 1821

According to the Constitution, one of four things a king can't give a president without consent of Congress

While we all remember Amy, this is the name of one of Jimmy Carter's other three kids

MOVIE CLASSICS

John Houseman said this title character was based partly on William Randolph Hearst and partly on Orson Welles

According to the title of an Errol Flynn film, "They" did this "with their boots on"

Cecil B. DeMille, Hedda Hopper, and Buster Keaton all played themselves in this Gloria Swanson classic

In *Gentleman's Agreement* he played a writer posing as a Jew to expose anti-Semitism

This duo co-starred in eight films, including *Blossoms in the Dust,* *Mrs. Miniver,* and *Madame Curie*

"NEW" ON THE MAP

Of all U.S. states beginning with "new," this one is alphabetically first

A Canadian province, or New Jersey home of Rutgers University

In 1977 voters elected Ernest N. "Dutch" Morial, the first black mayor of this city

This country, far from Holland, is named for a Dutch province

This French territory in the South Seas is named for Scotland

POP SINGERS

This "feline" South Carolinian starred on Broadway in *Timbuktu,* a black version of *Kismet*

Nightmarish singer who recorded "Welcome to My Nightmare"

Even though Meryl Streep rejected him in the movie *Plenty,* he didn't call the police

Oscar winner who led the singing of "God Bless America" at the end of 1988's Republican convention

Gilles Thibault wrote the original French lyrics to "My Way," and this man wrote the ones in English

DOLLS

Lots of people throw it away, but if it's in mint condition it may double the value of your doll

The 1976 "Baby Brother" Tender Love doll was controversial for this reason

In the mid-1800s china factories in this European country supplied nearly all dolls' heads and bodies worldwide

These five Canadian sisters, born in 1934, inspired dolls that are now collectors' items

Barbie has had a friend named Francie, a boyfriend named Ken, and a sister with this nautical name

ALL EARS

Living animal that has the largest ears

Nickname of the V-shaped indoor TV antenna

Made up of fat, it's the loosely hanging lower part of the auricle

Murine is the official brand of eardrops of this U.S. sports team

Of the five standard U.S. coins, the one on which you can see the right ear of a president

JEOPARDY!

PRESIDENTS	MOVIE CLASSICS	"NEW" ON THE MAP
Who was George Washington?	Who was *Citizen Kane?* (ACC: Charles Foster Kane)	What is New Hampshire?
Who is Jacqueline Kennedy Onassis or Frances Folsom Cleveland Presto?	What is "died"?	What is New Brunswick?
What is the Marine Band?	What is *Sunset Boulevard?*	What is New Orleans?
What is a present, emolument, office, or title?	Who is Gregory Peck?	What is New Zealand?
What is John (Jack), James (Chip), or Donnel (Jeff)?	Who were Greer Garson and Walter Pidgeon?	What is New Caledonia?

POP SINGERS	DOLLS	ALL EARS
Who is Eartha Kitt?	What is the (original) box it came in?	What is the (African) elephant?
Who is Alice Cooper?	What is it was anatomically correct?	What are rabbit ears?
Who is Sting?	What is Germany?	What is the earlobe?
Who is Shirley Jones?	Who are the Dionne Quintuplets?	What is the swim team?
Who is Paul Anka?	Who is Skipper?	What is the (Lincoln) penny?

DOUBLE JEOPARDY!

DRAMA

His play, *The Caine Mutiny Court-Martial,* was based on his own novel, *The Caine Mutiny*

In 1978 Vincent Price starred in a one-man show as this "Earnest" playwright

This play about Henry II and the Archbishop of Canterbury is subtitled "The Honor of God"

Susan Strasberg played the leading role in the original 1955 production of this play set in Amsterdam

The title character of this "maternal" Bertolt Brecht drama has a son named Swiss Cheese

EUROPEAN HISTORY

Before taking power, he was editor of the socialist paper *Avanti*

Of about 200, 700, or 1,200 years, length of time Ireland was ruled by England

He issued the October Manifesto during the 1905 revolution, but its promises went unfulfilled

When England's Queen Anne died, this German became king because he was a great grandson of James I

At the height of this war in 1870, some Frenchmen were so hungry they ate animals from the Paris zoo

ARCHITECTURE

A projecting support, whether or not it's "flying"

In architecture, it can be suspended over a statue; in furniture, it hangs above your bed

Found in classical architecture, a caryatid is a column shaped like this

Legend says the architect of this church on Red Square was blinded so he couldn't create another one

The oldest of the Greek classical orders, it featured the simplest capitals on the columns

BOOKS & AUTHORS

In his 80th year, the Paris street where he lived was renamed for this *Hunchback of Notre Dame* author

English tale of Mrs. Wickett and her boarder, an old schoolmaster from Brookfield Boys School

Dickens' unfinished last novel, he carried its solution to his grave

The military and the clergy are represented by the two colors in the title of this book by Stendhal

At the end of this Steinbeck novel, Danny's friends burn his house as a tribute to him

SCIENTISTS

German physicist who first used mercury in thermometers and invented a temperature scale

Son of a baron, he led teams that developed the V-2 rocket and launched the first U.S. satellite

This Persian poet wrote an algebra book and reformed the Muslim calendar

The "clicking" device that detects energetic subatomic particles is named for him

This Englishman is considered the most original and influential thinker in the history of science

THE THREE R'S

In mathematics they can be classified as real, irrational, or imaginary

It's also been called scrivener's palsy

To celebrate its 60th anniversary, this newspaper for schoolkids put out a retrospective book

Printing with this style of letters began in Venice about 1500

The subtitle of this 1955 book by Rudolf Flesch is "And What You Can Do About It"

DOUBLE JEOPARDY!

DRAMA	EUROPEAN HISTORY	ARCHITECTURE
Who is Herman Wouk?	Who was Benito Mussolini?	What is a buttress?
Who was Oscar Wilde?	What was about 700 years?	What is a canopy?
What is *Becket?*	Who was Nicholas II?	What is a woman?
What is *The Diary of Anne Frank?*	Who was George I?	What is St. Basil's?
What is *Mother Courage (and Her Children)?*	What was the Franco-Prussian War?	What is Doric?

BOOKS & AUTHORS	SCIENTISTS	THE THREE R'S
Who was Victor Hugo?	Who is (Gabriel Daniel) Fahrenheit?	What are numbers?
What is *Goodbye, Mr. Chips?*	Who is Wernher von Braun?	What is writers' cramp?
What is *The Mystery of Edwin Drood?*	Who is Omar Khayyám?	What is the *Weekly Reader?*
What is *The Red and the Black?*	Who is (Hans) Geiger?	What is italic?
What is *Tortilla Flat?*	Who was Sir Isaac Newton?	What is *Why Johnny Can't Read?*

FINAL JEOPARDY!

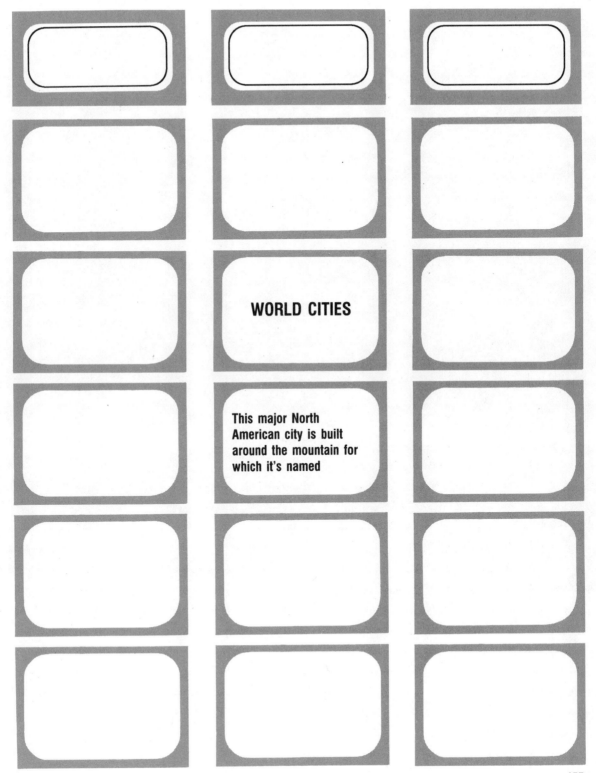

WORLD CITIES

This major North American city is built around the mountain for which it's named

FINAL JEOPARDY!

WORLD CITIES

What is Montreal?

Senior Tournament of Champions
#1

JEOPARDY!

WOMEN IN HISTORY

Lady Caroline Lamb was both Lord Byron's lover and the wife of William Lamb, this queen's first prime minister

Astronomer Maria Mitchell became world-famous after discovering one of these in 1847

In 1849 Elizabeth Blackwell became the first American woman to earn this degree

She married publisher George P. Putnam in 1931

This legendary Philadelphian was born Elizabeth Griscom in 1752 and wasn't famous until after her death

1988 MOVIES

In *18 Again,* this comic in his 90s switches bodies with his grandson

She played the human Wanda in *A Fish Called Wanda*

He played the bounty hunter hired to locate the accountant played by Charles Grodin

This actor played an actor playing a dictator in *Moon Over Parador*

In 1988 he starred in *Cocoon: The Return* and *Things Change,* and his name should ring a bell with you

PHILOSOPHERS

Though largely unknown when he died, he's been called the most prominent figure in Chinese history

Called "An outstanding thinker of the nineteenth century," this philosopher also wrote *War and Peace*

Rousseau said it's "a good bank account, a good cook, and a good digestion," Schulz, "a warm puppy"

Siegel and Shuster gave us the Superman of the comics, and he gave us the philosophical Superman

Aristocles was the real name of this Athenian known for his *Dialogues*

MUSICAL TEXAS TOWNS

Bing Crosby had a million seller about a rose in this third largest Texas town

In 1987 country music's George Strait went straight to this "yellow" Texas town "by morning"

In 1965 Dean Martin found himself "going back to" this city

It's how you would spell Dallas if you were singing a song from *The Most Happy Fella*

Chronologically speaking, Glen Campbell's hits went from Phoenix to Wichita to this city

GOLF

A number 3 wood, or what the dish ran away with

The site of the Ryder Cup match alternates between the U.S. and this country

Originally a nautical term for a channel between rocks, it's now the stretch between the tee and green

Possibly the greatest golfer of all time, he retired at 28 while still an amateur

Tony Lema earned his nickname when he bought this for the press after a tournament win

IN OTHER WORDS . . .

Business without recreation results in John being boring

Fire a pistol into a clock's mechanism

Drudgery enlarges encompassing all hours allotted

Agreeable employment, when obtainable

Make no inquiry, yours truly merely toils on these premises

JEOPARDY!

WOMEN IN HISTORY	1988 MOVIES	PHILOSOPHERS
Who was Queen Victoria?	Who is George Burns?	Who was Confucius?
What was a comet?	Who is Jamie Lee Curtis?	Who was (Count Leo) Tolstoy?
What is a medical degree?	Who is Robert de Niro?	What is happiness?
Who was Amelia Earhart?	Who is Richard Dreyfuss?	Who was (Friedrich) Nietzsche?
Who was Betsy Ross?	Who is Don Ameche?	Who was Plato?

MUSICAL TEXAS TOWNS	GOLF	IN OTHER WORDS . . .
What is San Antonio?	What is a spoon?	What is "All work and no play makes Jack a dull boy"?
What is Amarillo?	What is Great Britain?	What is "Shoot the works"? (ACC: killing time)
What is Houston?	What is the fairway?	What is "Work expands to fill the time available"?
What is "Big D—Little A—Double L—A—S"?	Who was Bobby Jones?	What is "Nice work, if you can get it"?
What is Galveston?	What is champagne?	What is "Don't ask me, I just work here"?

DOUBLE JEOPARDY!

NOVEL PLACES

The Admiral Benbow Inn near Black Hill Cove in the English countryside

Spanning a two and one-half month period, this novel begins and ends at London's Reform Club

Her life experiences take her from Gateshead Hall to Lowood School to Thornfield Manor

British Guiana and the densely forested area south of the Orinoco River in Venezuela

Floral Heights, on the outskirts of Zenith, a midwestern metropolis

BALLET

Though it's rarely done in ballet, Billy the Kid does this in Spanish in the ballet named for him

Historians say it was the *Ballet Comique de la Reine,* commissioned by Catherine de Médicis in 1581

Eighteenth-century ballet star Gaetano Vestris was known as "Dieu de la danse," which means this

This immortal nineteenth-century ballet tells the story of Albrecht's beloved, who still dances after her death

At the end of a Rimsky-Korsakov ballet, this title bird pecks the king to death

EVOLUTION

Proof that man walked upright 3.8 million years ago is seen in these in Tanzania, not Grauman's Chinese

The horseshoe crab is called a "living" one of these because it's changed little over 200 million years

The full title of Darwin's book is *On the Origin of Species by Means of* this

The Butler Act prohibiting the teaching of the theory of evolution was on this state's books until 1967

Modern man is the only living member of this species

PBS

The first black woman admitted to the University of Georgia, Charlayne Hunter-Gault is a correspondent on this "Newshour"

This science series, which premiered in March 1974, has featured such topics as "The Miracle of Life"

Host David McCullough takes PBS viewers on a journey through this museum's "World"

Host of "Wall Street Week" who posed for *Playboy* reading the *Wall St. Journal* in his pool

"Masterpiece Theatre"'s most popular and longest running presentation

WORLD CAPITALS

The two capitals on the island of Ireland are Dublin and this city

The world's highest ski run is on this country's Mount Chacaltaya near La Paz

The Organization of African Unity is headquartered in this capital of Ethiopia

Though Auckland was founded as New Zealand's capital, it soon lost the job to this city

Alphabetically first among Asian capitals, it's the capital of the United Arab Emirates

THE SUPREME COURT

It wasn't until 1869 that the number of justices stabilized at this number

He's the first Italian-American appointed to the Supreme Court

This president originally appointed Rehnquist to the Court as an associate justice

In 1969 this justice resigned amid criticism of his financial dealings

In July 1965 Arthur Goldberg resigned from the Court to accept this position

DOUBLE JEOPARDY!

NOVEL PLACES	BALLET	EVOLUTION
What is *Treasure Island?*	What is speak?	What are footprints?
What is *Around the World in 80 Days?*	What was the first ballet?	What is a (living) fossil?
Who is *Jane Eyre?*	What is the "God of the dance"?	What is *Natural Selection?*
What is *Green Mansions?*	What is *Giselle?*	What is Tennessee?
What is *Babbitt?* (ACC: *Dodsworth*)	What is *Le Coq d'Or?* (ACC: *The Golden Cockerel*)	What is *Homo sapiens*?

PBS	WORLD CAPITALS	THE SUPREME COURT
What is "The MacNeil-Lehrer Newshour"?	What is Belfast?	What is nine?
What is "Nova"?	What is Bolivia?	Who is Antonin Scalia?
What is the Smithsonian?	What is Addis Ababa?	Who is Nixon?
Who is Louis Rukeyser?	What is Wellington?	Who is Abe Fortas?
What was "Upstairs, Downstairs"?	What is Abu Dhabi?	What is U.N. Ambassador?

FINAL JEOPARDY!

AMERICAN POETS

He wrote a biography that won a Pulitzer prize for history in 1940 and won for his poetry in 1951

FINAL JEOPARDY!

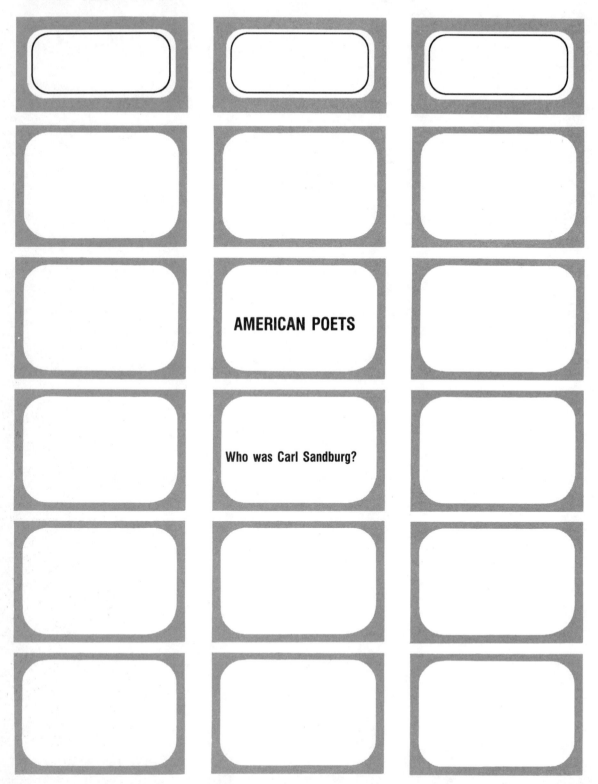

AMERICAN POETS

Who was Carl Sandburg?

Senior Tournament of Champions
#2

JEOPARDY!

MYTHOLOGY

A greedy king, or a brand of automobile muffler

The muse of history, or an award given for the best advertisements of the year

The Greek goddess of victory, or a brand of athletic shoe

The sea nymph who loved Odysseus, or a type of Caribbean folk music

A priestess of Aphrodite, or a kind of sandwich

PROVERBS

As you do this, "so you must lie on it," which is hard to do if you think about it

"There is a remedy for all things but" this

"Gold goes in at any gate, except," this one

According to Dickens, these will happen even in "the best-regulated families"

In "Lady Clara Vere de Vere," Tennyson wrote, "Kind hearts are more than" these

THE ENVIRONMENT

On a single day, a satellite counted 7,603 fires burning in the rain forests of this river basin

The EPA is planning to extinguish all new use of this carcinogenic fire retardant

The 125-foot Sebrell elm, the largest in the U.S., is dying of this fungus disease

Du Pont recently announced it would stop manufacturing chlorofluorocarbons because they damage this

In 1988 a canine virus killed thousands of these marine mammals near the coast of Europe

ACTORS OF THE PAST

In 1895 Henry Irving became the first British actor to receive this honor

Stage name of Emilie Charlotte Le Breton, the "Jersey Lily"

Historically, this ancient Greek is considered the very first actor

Born Maude Kiskadden in Utah in 1872, she was best known for playing Peter Pan

George Bernard Shaw wrote the part of Eliza Doolittle for this actress, whom he reportedly loved

SING "OUT"

"I get no kick from champagne," wrote Cole Porter in this classic from *Anything Goes*

In 1941's *Ziegfeld Girl* Tony Martin sang "You stepped . . ."

A 1932 Rudy Vallee hit said "Let's" do this "and go to sleep"

Song that says, "I want you to want me, I need you so badly, I can't think of anything but you"

1970 Diana Ross hit also heard at the 1984 summer Olympics opening ceremonies

THE FIVE & DIME

Barbara Hutton's granddad, his New York skyscraper was built on your parents' nickels and dimes

This five-and-dimer is the "K" in Kmart

Chenille stems, which are better known as these, are one of the few items you can still buy for a dime

Giant star whose name completes the title "Come Back to the Five-and-Dime . . ."

According to the song, it's what Ronald Reagan "found" in a 1941 film in "a five-and-ten-cent store"

JEOPARDY!

MYTHOLOGY

Who is Midas?

Who is Clio?

Who is Nike?

What is Calypso?

Who is Hero?

PROVERBS

What is "Make your bed"?

What is death?

What is Heaven's?

What are accidents?

What are coronets?

THE ENVIRONMENT

What is the Amazon?

What is asbestos?

What is Dutch elm disease?

What is the ozone layer?

What are seals?

ACTORS OF THE PAST	SING "OUT"	THE FIVE & DIME
What is being knighted?	What is "I Get a Kick Out of You"?	Who was Frank W. Woolworth?
What was Lillie Langtry?	What is "out of a dream"?	Who was Sebastian S. Kresge?
Who was Thespis?	What is "put out the lights"?	What are pipe cleaners?
Who was Maude Adams?	What is "Goin' Out of My Head"?	Who is *Jimmy Dean (Jimmy Dean)*?
Who was Mrs. Patrick Campbell?	What is "Reach Out and Touch Somebody's Hand"?	What is a "million dollar baby"?

DOUBLE JEOPARDY!

FOUR-LETTER WORDS

Christmas, or a large log traditionally burned at that time

To do this involves the respiratory muscles and may be caused by watching others do it

The two four-letter weapons you can fence with

To push your wares in the streets, or a bird of prey of the order Falconiformes

From the metaphor of the church as a ship, the term for this part of a church is from Latin for "ship"

BOTANY

Speculation in these bulbs in Holland in the seventeenth century caused financial chaos

Called gum trees in Australia, these tall flowering trees provide oil for medicine and leaves for koalas

After creating the boysenberry, Rudolph Boysen gave his vines to this founder of a California amusement park

When talking about plants it means a disease caused by certain fungi, not dirty pictures

For flowers, it's considered the first stage in the reproductive process

U.S. HISTORY

Around 1839 the old State House bell came to be known as this

Henry Cabot Lodge led the fight to keep the U.S. from joining this after WWI

On January 3, 1777, General Washington's forces captured Nassau Hall, this college's administration building

In 1870 David Dixon Porter became the second U.S. admiral; this man, his adopted brother, was the first

In 1976's "Koreagate," the Justice Department investigated this South Korean businessman

CLASSICAL MUSICIANS

Born in Paris, this noted Chinese cellist is a real "yo-yo"

This brilliant Israeli-American violinist is an avid New York Knicks fan

This late classical conductor wrote the music for the film *On the Waterfront* as well as *West Side Story*

Famed for his 18-karat gold flute, this Irish flautist had a hit playing John Denver's "Annie's Song"

In 1966 cellist Mstislav Rostropovich said the right person to carry on his work was this 21-year-old British virtuosa

WORLD GEOGRAPHY

Europe is a huge peninsula that extends westward from this continent

This country, at the outlet of the Ganges and two other major rivers, had severe floods in September 1988

Two of the four major islands of Indonesia, together they form the Greater Sunda Islands

Africa's highest peak, Mt. Kilimanjaro, is in this country

The term "banana republic" originally referred to this Central American country

LITERARY TERMS

It can be a collection of three works by one author or three by different authors with a common theme

This type of verse is also called unrhymed iambic pentameter

Latin for "a great work," it's a major literary work, or a writer's masterpiece

In literature, it's not artillery but a body of writings established as authentic

Term for writings of doubtful authority that's applied to some books associated with the Bible

DOUBLE JEOPARDY!

FOUR-LETTER WORDS

What is Yule?

What is yawn?

What are a foil and an epée?

What is hawk?

What is a nave?

BOTANY

What are tulip bulbs?

What are eucalyptus trees?

Who was Walter Knott?

What is smut?

What is pollination?

U.S. HISTORY

What is the Liberty Bell?

What is the League of Nations?

What is Princeton?

Who was David Farragut?

Who is Tongsun Park? (ACC: Park Tong Sun)

CLASSICAL MUSICIANS	WORLD GEOGRAPHY	LITERARY TERMS
Who is Yo-Yo Ma?	What is Asia?	What is a trilogy?
Who is Itzhak Perlman?	What is Bangladesh?	What is blank verse?
Who was Leonard Bernstein?	What are Java, Sumatra, Celebes, and Kalimantan (Borneo)?	What is a magnum opus?
Who is James Galway?	What is Tanzania?	What is a canon?
Who was Jacqueline du Pré?	What is Honduras?	What are Apocrypha?

FINAL JEOPARDY!

MONARCHS

Berengaria, who never set foot in England, was its queen for eight years after marrying this king on Cyprus

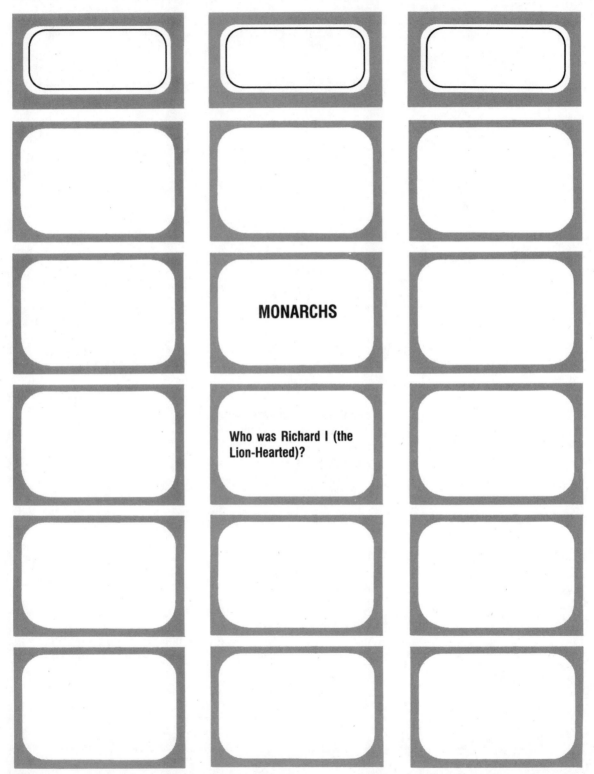

MONARCHS

Who was Richard I (the Lion-Hearted)?

College Tournament of Champions
#1

JEOPARDY!

BUSINESS & INDUSTRY

This Viacom music television format broadcasts in many countries

In 1989 an Oscar was given to this film manufacturer in honor of its 100 years in the industry

Memphis-based overnight delivery service that now has 10,000 drop-off boxes similar to mailboxes

In February 1989 Sears closed over 800 stores for 42 hours to do this

Centered around Seventh Avenue, it's New York City's largest manufacturing industry

PATRON SAINTS

Though St. Jerome is patron saint of these people, they'll still fine you if you return his works overdue

Just the facts, ma'am; his name's Michael, he's a saint, the patron saint of these

Of Vanity, Apollonia, or Sheila E., the patron saint of dentists and toothache sufferers

St. James may not have been as mad as one, but he is a patron saint of them

She's the patron saint of miners, not of an NBC soap opera

COUNTRIES

Among the regions in this country are Old Castile, New Castile, and Andalusia

Country whose capital includes Buda on the west bank of the Danube and Pest on the east

Though not part of the Organization of American States, it's the largest country in area in the Americas

This city at the foot of the Pichincha volcano is Ecuador's capital

The name of this West African country means "lion mountains"

COLLEGE TRIVIA

Students at Boston College can get their grades from machines like these you'd find at your bank

Transylvania University, oldest U.S. college west of the Alleghenies, is in Lexington in this state

This group that featured Lionel Richie got its start at Tuskegee University

The NCAA's proposition 42 calls for at least a 700 SAT score and this GPA to win a first-year athletic scholarship

When students protested his membership on the board of this mostly black D.C. university, Lee Atwater resigned

FOUR-LETTER WORDS

The underside part of the hand extending from the wrist to the base of the fingers

Already gone, it's not right

This word meaning to breathe in short gasps comes from the same root as "fantasy"

It can precede baby, league, or whacker

To draw straight, parallel lines on a paper, or make a decision in court

COOKING

This beef stroganoff ingredient can be "sour" or "whipping"

This ground-beef dish was named for J. Salisbury, a physician who advocated dietary reform

To make chicken à la this, you usually need mushrooms and pimientos

Quite simply, this is melted butter with the sediment removed

The name of this French dish means "pot on the fire"

JEOPARDY!

BUSINESS & INDUSTRY	PATRON SAINTS	COUNTRIES
What is MTV?	What are librarians?	What is Spain?
What is Kodak?	What are policemen?	What is Hungary?
What is Federal Express?	Who is St. Apollonia?	What is Canada?
What is lower prices? (ACC: take inventory)	What are hatters?	What is Quito?
What is the garment industry?	Who is St. Barbara?	What is Sierra Leone?

COLLEGE TRIVIA	FOUR-LETTER WORDS	COOKING
What are ATMs?	What is the palm?	What is cream?
What is Kentucky?	What is left?	What is Salisbury steak?
What are the Commodores?	What is pant?	What is (chicken à la) king?
What is a 2.0?	What is bush?	What is clarified butter? (ACC: drawn butter or ghee)
What is Howard University?	What is rule?	What is pot au feu?

DOUBLE JEOPARDY!

IN THE NEWS

On April 7, 1989, a Soviet nuclear-powered submarine sank near this Scandinavian country

In February 1989 Jimmy Johnson was hired to replace him as coach of the Dallas Cowboys

This man shot Ronald Reagan, James Brady, and two security men in March 1981

Robert McFarlane became the first government official sentenced for his role in this

On February 10, 1989, this Washington, D.C., attorney became the first black to chair the Democratic party

THE BRAIN

A mnemonic device helps you improve this

In this stage of sleep the brain is alert, but most of your muscles are in a paralyzed state

Reader's Digest reports there is no correlation between the size of one's brain and this

Each hemisphere is divided into four of these, the temporal, occipital, parietal, and frontal

Encephalitis is an inflammation of the brain, and this is an inflammation of the membrane surrounding it

NOVELS

D. H. Lawrence could have called this book *Oliver Mellors' Lover*

Kimball O'Hara is the central character in this Kipling novel

George Orwell's two most famous books, they were the last novels he wrote

Remarque said the purpose of this novel was "to tell of a generation of men . . . destroyed by" WWI

Her first novel was *The Heart Is a Lonely Hunter*

AMERICAN HISTORY

This Treasury Department agency was founded in 1865 to catch counterfeiters, not to protect the president

At one time, six white beads of this Indian currency were worth one English penny

Evangelist Billy Sunday said, "Goodbye, John Barleycorn" when this was passed in 1919

When Washington crossed the Delaware, he went from Pennsylvania to this state

Hannibal Hamlin was his first vice president

POTPOURRI

His $25,000 sports car with a stainless-steel finish and gull-wing doors was built in Northern Ireland

Of mollusks, algae, or dinosaurs, the last to appear on earth

Of the four sections in a typical orchestra, the one that includes the most musicians

Two of the six U.N. members whose names begin with the letter "L"

Of the planets in our solar system, this one is last alphabetically

DISNEY DOGS

A bloodhound chasing Mickey in *The Chain Gang,* he later became "Mickey's pal"

He began in the early 1930s as a stringbean character called Dippy Dawg

In 1960 the new xerography process made it unnecessary for the animators to draw all 101 of these

Walt Disney's first live-action comedy and his first to star Fred MacMurray

In a 1957 film, this dog fights off a pack of wild pigs

DOUBLE JEOPARDY!

IN THE NEWS	THE BRAIN	NOVELS
What is Norway?	What is your memory?	What is *Lady Chatterley's Lover?*
Who is Tom Landry?	What is REM (rapid eye movement) sleep?	What is *Kim?*
Who is John Hinckley (Jr.)?	What is intelligence?	What are *Animal Farm* and *1984?*
What is the Iran-Contra affair?	What are lobes?	What is *All Quiet on the Western Front?*
Who is Ronald H. Brown?	What is meningitis?	Who was Carson McCullers?

AMERICAN HISTORY	POTPOURRI	DISNEY DOGS
What is the Secret Service?	Who is John DeLorean?	Who is Pluto?
What is wampum?	What were dinosaurs?	Who is Goofy?
What is Prohibition or the 18th Amendment? (ACC: Volstead Act)	What is the string section?	What are dalmatians?
What is New Jersey?	What are Laos, Lebanon, Lesotho, Liberia, Libya, and/or Luxembourg?	What is *The Shaggy Dog?*
Who is Abraham Lincoln?	What is Venus?	What is *Old Yeller?*

FINAL JEOPARDY!

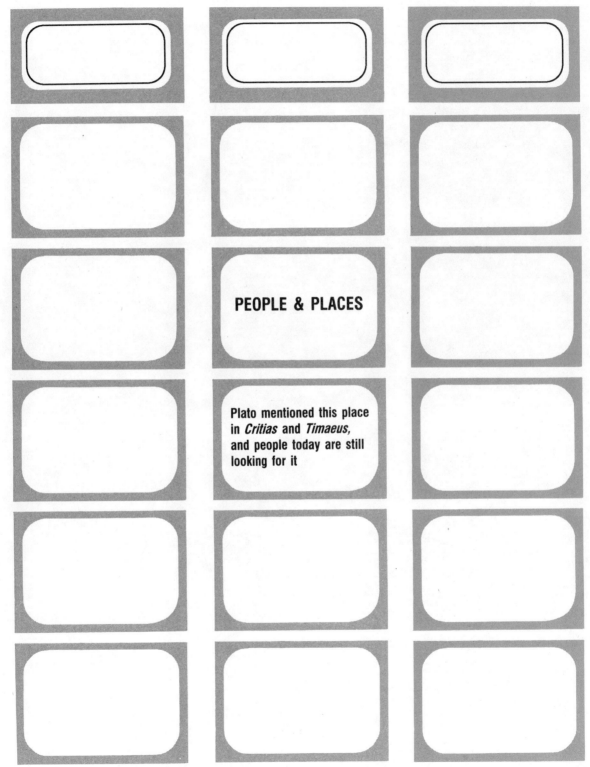

PEOPLE & PLACES

Plato mentioned this place in *Critias* and *Timaeus,* and people today are still looking for it

FINAL JEOPARDY!

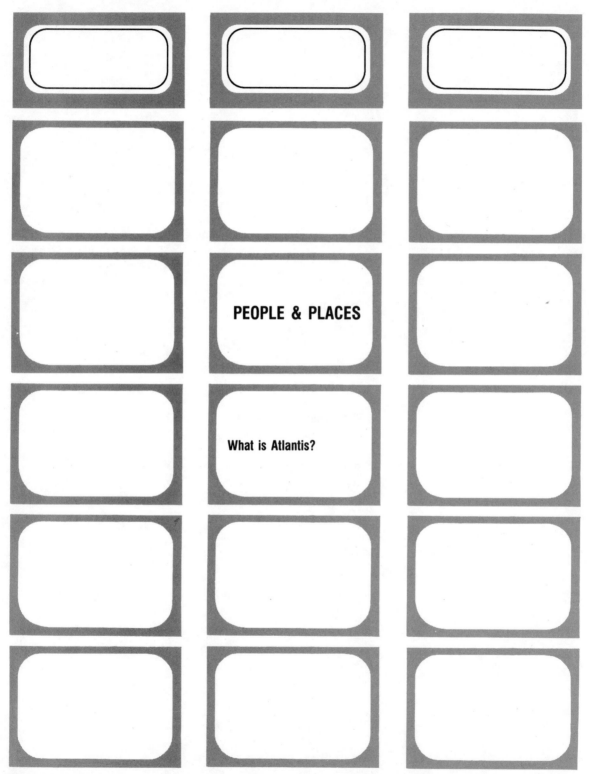

PEOPLE & PLACES

What is Atlantis?

College Tournament of Champions
#2

JEOPARDY!

STARTS WITH "B"

Despite its name, you don't have to be single to earn one of these degrees

It commonly precedes hound, lust, and sucker

In ancient Egypt both kings and queens wore false metal ones as a sign of sovereignty

This word can refer to an Irish accent or an Irish shoe

A glass vessel designed to cover and protect, it's also the title of a Sylvia Plath novel

BIRDS

The ancient Romans thought this TV network symbol a great delicacy roasted and served in its feathers

A 56-foot one of these atop a fast food restaurant in Marietta, Georgia, is a local landmark

Branch of zoology that's the scientific study of birds

The most expensive commercial leather from a bird comes from this one

The name of this chattering crow is partly from a nickname for Margaret

SEE THE USA

Famous home, now a museum, that's located on Elvis Presley Boulevard in Memphis, Tennessee

You can see Mister Rogers' sweater and this TV character's leather jacket at the Smithsonian

London Bridge was falling down, so it was moved and rebuilt in this state's Lake Havasu City

The famous 17-mile drive is located on this California peninsula

Signs warning hikers in these New Hampshire mountains say, "Stop. The area ahead has the worst weather in America."

PSYCHOLOGY

Carl Jung thought this "father of psychoanalysis" had a father complex

This term for thought-reform through propaganda and intimidation is from the Korean War era

Pavlov's dogs exhibited this conditioned reflex at the sound of a bell

French for "already seen," it's that funny feeling you've lived through something before

The false belief that everybody's picking on you

FASHION HISTORY

In the 1700s fashionable men wore three-cornered ones

The cardinal was a hooded cloak of this color, as its name suggests

This fancy term for ladies' underwear comes from the Latin meaning "made of linen"

Short skirts, bobbed hair, and extremely low waistlines first came into style in the U.S. during this decade

Elizabethans wore rabatos, which were wide, lace-edged ones stiffened to stand up high in the back

THE SPORT PLAYED

Mark Roth, Marshall Holman, and Nelson Burton, Jr.

Matt Biondi, Janet Evans, and Kristin Otto

José Canseco, Roger Clemens, and Darryl Strawberry

Eric Dickerson, Bernie Kosar, and Joe Montana

Rick Mears, Bobby Allison, and Richard Petty

JEOPARDY!

STARTS WITH "B"	BIRDS	SEE THE USA
What is a bachelor or bachelor's degree?	What is a peacock?	What is Graceland?
What is blood?	What is a chicken?	Who is the Fonz or Fonzie?
What were beards?	What is ornithology?	What is Arizona?
What is a brogue?	What is the ostrich?	What is Monterey?
What is a bell jar?	What is magpie?	What are the White Mountains?

PSYCHOLOGY	FASHION HISTORY	THE SPORT PLAYED
Who is (Sigmund) Freud?	What are hats?	What is bowling?
What is brainwashing?	What is scarlet? (ACC: red)	What is swimming?
What is salivation?	What is lingerie?	What is baseball?
What is déjà vu?	What was the 1920s?	What is football?
What is paranoia?	What are collars?	What is auto racing?

DOUBLE JEOPARDY!

PRESIDENTS

Wilson was our last president born in Virginia, and he was our first

He was the first president to serve only one term

While serving as this man's vice president, Aaron Burr killed Alexander Hamilton

Teddy Roosevelt became president upon his assassination

The only president whose father was a signer of the Declaration of Independence

ENGLISH LITERATURE

He wrote *Chitty Chitty Bang Bang*, a children's story, as well as the James Bond novels

This country's 1930s civil war was the setting for Graham Greene's *The Confidential Agent*

The title of this 1872 Samuel Butler novel, published anonymously, is an anagram for "nowhere"

Mr. Lockwood, a tenant of Thrushcross Grange, narrates this Emily Brontë story

Her first novel, *Sense and Sensibility,* was published two years before *Pride and Prejudice*

TECHNOLOGY

Each year, Idaho sends samples of this crop to California's Camp Pendleton to be tested for disease

Also called an electronic oven, it uses high-frequency electromagnetic waves to heat food

An architectural technique called base isolation uses rubber and steel pads to absorb waves from these

In 1978 the *Double Eagle II* became the first gas-filled craft of this type to cross the Atlantic

Some 85 percent of water used in the western U.S. is used for this purpose

LAKES & RIVERS

If the new London Bridge in England, not Arizona, fell down, it would fall into this river

To get to Paris' Notre Dame Cathedral you have to cross a bridge over this river

This lake on the Manitoba-Saskatchewan border sounds like a watering hole for Santa's sleigh team

During the sixteenth century, Ivan IV claimed all of this great river's valley for Russia

Though the Nile is longer, this second-longest river in Africa carries more water

CLASSICAL MUSIC

Type of fairy that Tchaikovsky set a-dancing in *The Nutcracker*

The "Hallelujah Chorus" is found at the end of Part II of this Handel work

Bach's set of repetitive pieces designed to show contrapuntal technique is called *The Art of* this

Haydn's Symphony No. 83 is called the *Hen* from its "clucking," and his No. 101 this from its "ticking"

This composer died before finishing *The Tales of Hoffmann;* Ernest Guiraud finished it

FAMOUS STUDENTS

She was at UCLA on a basketball scholarship when Bob Kersee discovered her track and field talents

At his academy he reiterated what he'd learned from Socrates and sometimes adapted his ideas

He studied directing at NYU under Martin Scorsese and was an "absolutely mahvelous" student

At Cornell, *Gravity's Rainbow* author Thomas Pynchon studied under this author of *Lolita*

Mark van Doren and Lionel Trilling both taught this "howl"ing poet when he studied at Columbia

DOUBLE JEOPARDY!

PRESIDENTS	ENGLISH LITERATURE	TECHNOLOGY
Who was George Washington?	Who was Ian Fleming?	What are potatoes?
Who was John Adams?	What is Spain?	What is a microwave oven?
Who was Thomas Jefferson?	What is *Erewhon?*	What are earthquakes?
Who was William McKinley?	What is *Wuthering Heights?*	What is a balloon?
Who was John Quincy Adams?	Who was Jane Austen?	What is irrigation?

LAKES & RIVERS

What is the Thames?

What is the Seine?

What is Reindeer Lake?

What is the Volga?

What is the Congo?
(ACC: Zaire River)

CLASSICAL MUSIC

What is a sugarplum fairy?

What is the *Messiah?*

What is *Fugue?*

What is the *Clock* Symphony?

Who was Jacques Offenbach?

FAMOUS STUDENTS

Who is Jackie Joyner-Kersee?

Who is Plato?

Who is Billy Crystal?

Who was Vladimir Nabokov?

Who is Allen Ginsberg?

FINAL JEOPARDY!

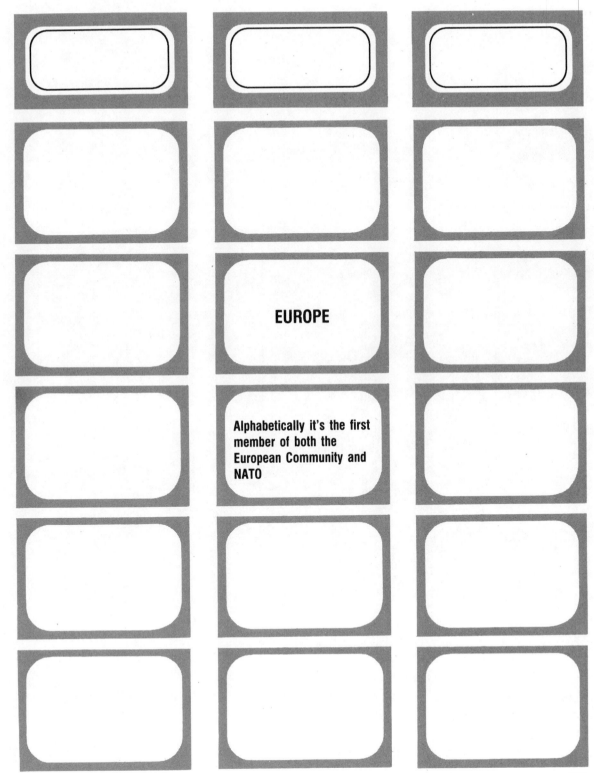

EUROPE

Alphabetically it's the first member of both the European Community and NATO

FINAL JEOPARDY!

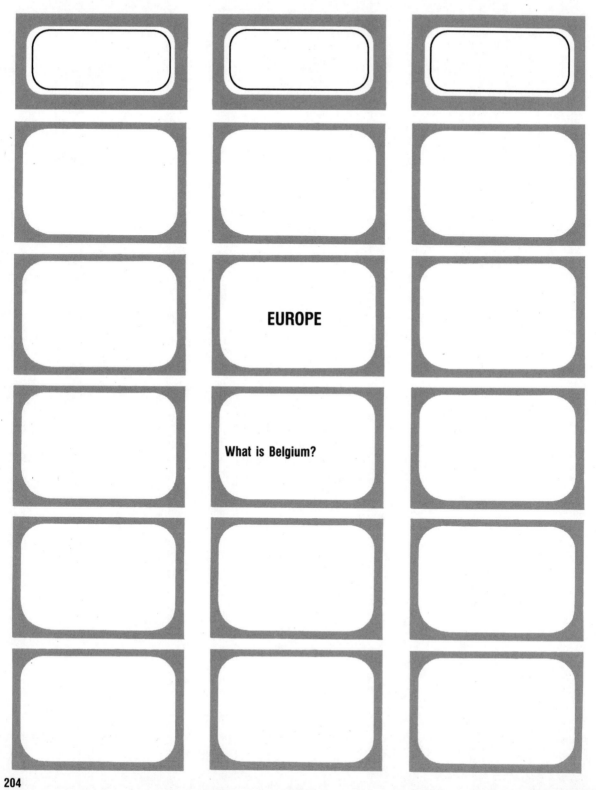

EUROPE

What is Belgium?

Teen Tournament of Champions #1

JEOPARDY!

WORD ORIGINS

The "acu" in acupuncture comes from the Latin for these instruments used in acupuncture

A large tomb is called this because of the majestic one built for King Mausolus in the fourth century B.C.

Originally made in Nîmes, France, this fabric was called *serge denimes*

This rodent's name comes from Middle French for "spiny pig"

From the Latinized form of his last name, a "Shavian" is a fan of this man

TEEN CUISINE

This national hamburger chain's patties are square, but the buns are still round

The best-selling diet soda in the U.S. with about 11.5 percent of the soft drink market

A variety of Hostess Twinkies now comes with this fruit mixed with the creme filling

Ralston Purina's donut-shaped cereal sold in chocolate and glazed varieties is named for this donut chain

E.T. created a sales boom for this candy

AMERICAN HISTORY

This president's five-year-old son died in 1864 after falling from a porch in Richmond

This wild frontiersman's first and middle names were James Butler; where Bill came from isn't known

In early New England, wearing the letter "A" was one punishment for this

Samuel Sewall was the only judge at these colonial trials who later repented publicly

In 1848 Lucretia Mott and Elizabeth Cady Stanton held the first U.S. convention to promote this

THE METRIC SYSTEM	MUSICALS IN OTHER WORDS	"FUN" STUFF
Everyday temperature measurements in the metric system are made using this scale	"Merry-go-round"	Something that produces an enjoyment level greater than primates in a keg is said to be this
Speedometers on most cars in the U.S. can be read in either miles per hour or these	"Felines"	In a popular carol, line that follows "Jingle all the way!"
The prefix meaning thousandfold is kilo-, and thousandth part this	"Miss Oakley grab that firearm"	Title of Cyndi Lauper's 1984 hit, which made her a star
The meter was first defined as one ten-millionth of the distance between this point and the equator	"Greetings, Mrs. Levi!"	According to the commercial, the two things chewing Doublemint gum can do for you
A group of scientists in this country set up the metric system in the 1790s	"The 46th state!"	Frivolously diverting activity, when you're grounded there's no more of this famous pair, buster

JEOPARDY!

WORD ORIGINS	TEEN CUISINE	AMERICAN HISTORY
What are the needles?	What is Wendy's?	Who was Jefferson Davis?
What is a mausoleum?	What is Diet Coke?	Who was Wild Bill Hickok?
What is denim?	What is strawberry?	What is adultery?
What is a porcupine?	What is Dunkin' Donuts?	What were the Salem (witchcraft) Trials?
Who was George Bernard Shaw?	What are Reese's Pieces?	What are women's rights?

THE METRIC SYSTEM	MUSICALS IN OTHER WORDS	"FUN" STUFF

What is the Celsius scale? (ACC: centrigrade)

What is *Carousel?*

What is ("It's) more fun than a barrel full of monkeys"?

What are kilometers per hour?

What is *Cats?*

What is "Oh, what fun it is to ride in a one-horse open sleigh!"?

What is milli-?

What is *Annie Get Your Gun?*

What is "Girls Just Want to Have Fun"?

What is the North Pole?

What is *Hello, Dolly!?*

What is double your pleasure and double your fun?

What is France?

What is *Oklahoma!?*

What is fun and games?

209

DOUBLE JEOPARDY!

PREHISTORIC BEASTS

This "tyrant lizard king" was the most feared meat-eater of its time

The lovely triceratops had three of these on its face

Many of these flying reptiles had a wingspan about five times that of a bald eagle

Dinosaurs lived during this era, the age of reptiles

All dinosaurs classed as *sauropods* had this number of toes on each foot, like modern lizards

FICTION

Number of gables in the title house of a Nathaniel Hawthorne novel

In this novel, Holden Caulfield says Stradlater, his roommate, is a secret slob who shaves with a rusty razor

Passepartout is the French valet who travels with Phileas Fogg in this Jules Verne novel

New England state mentioned in the title of a Mark Twain novel, he also lived there

Apocalypse Now was based on this author's *Heart of Darkness*

MONTHS

This month has charm and is also an anagram of it

One of two major religions whose calendars contain months of only 29 or 30 days

Pronounced one way it means majestic, pronounced this way, a month

Total number of days in all the months whose names end in "ber"

When the normal Roman calendar was expanded from 10 to 12 months, these were the two that were added

MEDICINE

This type of surgery was named for the way Julius Caesar supposedly was born

This worm lives in beef muscle and can infest the human intestinal tract

Gingivitis is an inflammation of this part of the body caused by poor nutrition or hygiene

This disease, which can affect many muscles, not just those of the mouth, is also called lockjaw

Overactivity in this gland found in the neck can cause hot flashes, weight loss, and rapid heartbeat

CINEMATIC SPECTERS

The director of this 1988 Christmas film said he wanted the wires that lifted Carol Kane to be visible

Geena Davis and Alec Baldwin haunted their own house in this 1988 hit film

Seen briefly in *Ghostbusters,* this little green guy is featured in the TV cartoon series

Steven Spielberg co-wrote and co-produced this first of three films about the Freeling clan's ghost trouble

Her list of roles includes a mermaid, a cave woman, and in 1988's *High Spirits,* a ghost

NATIONAL PARKS

Lake Windermere, this country's largest lake, is located in its Lake District National Park

Ye gods! You'll find Olympus National Park in this country

Ibex goats range in the peaks of Schweizerische National Park in this country

Pre-Columbian cliff and cave dwellings can be found in Mesa Verde National Park in this country

This country's Ujung-Kulon nature reserve is a refuge for the Javan tiger and Javan rhino

DOUBLE JEOPARDY!

PREHISTORIC BEASTS	FICTION	MONTHS
What was the *Tyrannosaurus rex?*	What is seven?	What is March?
What are horns?	What is *The Catcher in the Rye?*	What is Judaism or Islam?
What were pterodactyls?	What is *Around the World in 80 Days?*	What is August?
What is the Mesozoic era?	What is Connecticut?	What is 122?
What is five?	Who is Joseph Conrad?	What are January and February?

MEDICINE	CINEMATIC SPECTERS	NATIONAL PARKS
What is a caesarean section?	What is *Scrooged?*	What is England?
What is a tapeworm?	What is *Beetlejuice?*	What is Greece?
What are the gums? (ACC: mouth)	Who is Slimer?	What is Switzerland?
What is tetanus?	What is *Poltergeist?*	What is the U.S.?
What is the thyroid?	Who is Daryl Hannah?	What is Indonesia?

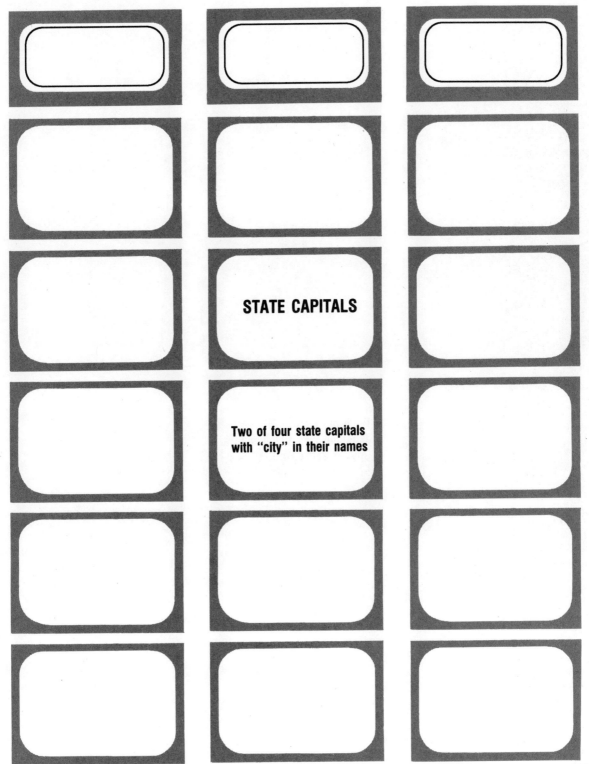

STATE CAPITALS

Two of four state capitals with "city" in their names

FINAL JEOPARDY!

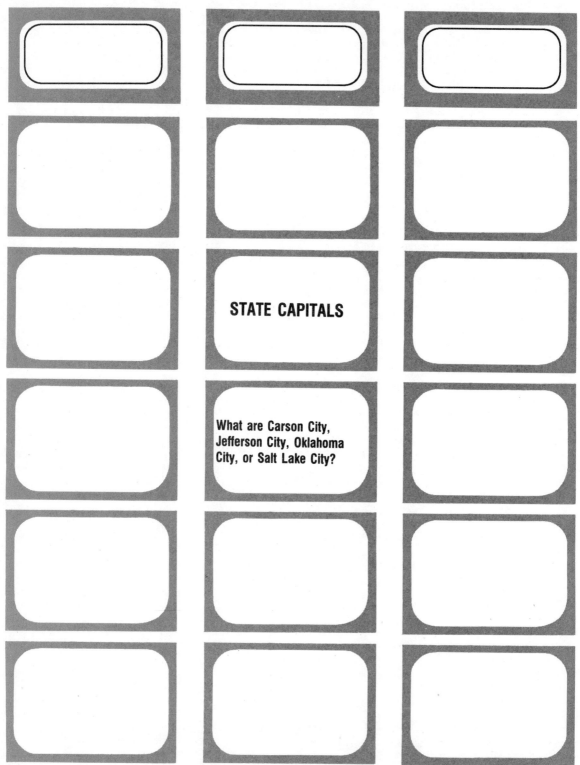

STATE CAPITALS

What are Carson City, Jefferson City, Oklahoma City, or Salt Lake City?

Teen Tournament of Champions #2

JEOPARDY!

WHAT'S IN A NAME

Perhaps the most common name in Christian countries, variations include May and Marilyn

Anglo-Saxon for "the rich, happy, and prosperous," ask Mrs. Bunker

Celtic for "dweller by the waterfall," or a TV series about dwellers at Southfork

"Warrior" in Slavic, it could be a Badenov or a Karloff

The face of this Greek "light" launched a thousand ships

MATH

A number system using a base of 10, Dewey used one to catalogue library books

Proportionally, 3 is to 4 as 75 is to this number

The study of 3-dimensional objects, it sounds like a substantial math course

If triangle ABC is equal in size and shape to triangle XYZ, they are said to be this

If a sales tax is 6.5 percent, you'd spend a total of this much for a $4 item

WORLD CAPITALS

Only about 4,000 people lived in this Greek city when it was recaptured from the Turks in 1833

This Asian city needed major rebuilding after the earthquake and fire of 1923, and again after WWII

Via del Corso, the main street of this capital, is named for the horse races once run there

The golden stupa in the Shwe Dagon Pagoda is the most notable building in this city Burmese call Yangon

In this Arab capital, Christians live mainly on the east side and Muslims mainly on the west side

EVERYDAY INVENTIONS

C. Latham Sholes invented this—not Olivetti or Smith or even Corona

Clarence Birdseye got the idea for frozen food after living among these people for three years

Of Dunlop, Goodyear, or Goodrich, the veterinarian who invented the pneumatic bike tire

This, not corn, was used to make the Kellogg brothers' first flakes

The first lightweight one for home use consisted of a fan motor, a soap box, a broom handle, and a pillowcase

FISH

A shark may use over 20,000 of these in a lifetime, since they're replaced when worn out

The paddlefish is found in this U.S. river famous for its paddleboats

The name of the game fish known as the pickerel is a diminutive of the name of this game fish

About 1400, a Dutch fisherman found a way to cure and barrel these fish, which became a major item of trade

Cave fish have either very minute ones or ones that are totally inoperative

STATE NAMES

Literally, this Hoosier state is the "Land of the Indians"

Previously named for France's Charles IX, these two states were renamed for England's Charles I

Its name is probably from the Algonquian for "great river"

Since the Spanish discovered this state on Easter Sunday, 1513, they called it "Flowery Easter"

It's not certain from where this New England state got its name, but it wasn't from the Indians

JEOPARDY!

WHAT'S IN A NAME	MATH	WORLD CAPITALS
What is Mary?	What is decimal?	What is Athens?
What is Edith?	What is 100?	What is Tokyo?
What is Dallas?	What is solid geometry?	What is Rome?
What is Boris?	What is congruent?	What is Rangoon?
Who is Helen?	What is $4.26?	What is Beirut?

EVERYDAY INVENTIONS	FISH	STATE NAMES
What is a typewriter?	What are teeth?	What is Indiana?
What are the Eskimos?	What is the Mississippi?	What are North and South Carolina?
Who was John Dunlop?	What is the pike?	What is Mississippi?
What is wheat?	What are herring?	What is Florida?
What is a vacuum cleaner?	What are eyes?	What is Maine?

DOUBLE JEOPARDY!

EXPLORERS

In 1520 this explorer found a strait just north of Tierra del Fuego

In full armor, sword in hand, banner of Castile in the other, he waded into the Pacific in 1513

In 1487 Bartolomeu Dias rounded the southern tip of this continent

This noted sponsor of explorers was the third son of Portugal's King John I

Founded in 1608 by Champlain as a fur trading post, it was the capital city of New France

FIRST LADIES

She was valedictorian of her high school class in Plains, Georgia

Martha Washington is buried at this national shrine in Fairfax County, Virginia

Aaron Burr introduced this lady to our future fourth president

Tina Turner said this glamorous First Lady was always her role model

Mary Tyler Moore played this Mary in a 1988 TV mini-series

EUROPE

This mountain chain, older than the Alps, contains the town of Lourdes, a pilgrimage center

You must pass the Matura exam to attend one of this country's universities in Graz, Salzburg, or Innsbruck

Common name of the treaty the former Soviet Union and six of its satellites signed in Poland in May 1955

The state of New Jersey was named after the island of Jersey in this group between England and France

The names of its two official languages are both found within the name of this eastern European country

NURSERY RHYMES

When Simple Simon met the pieman, he was going to this event

The answer to this question is "three bags full"

"Hickety pickety, my black hen, she" does this "for gentlemen"

As far as we know, it's the only thing that conceited Little Jack Horner ever said

"As I was going to St. Ives, I met a man with" this many wives

NUCLEAR PHYSICS

Nuclear energy is released when this part of the atom is split

Radioactive elements give off three kinds of rays named for these Greek letters

Martin Klaproth named this element he discovered in 1789 in honor of a planet found eight years earlier

If an element has 26 protons, 30 neutrons, and 26 electrons, this is its atomic number

It occurs in the core of a reactor when the cooling system fails and temperatures rise above 5,000°F

HODGEPODGE

In 1988 this nautical character wore a Santa suit on boxes of his Christmas crunch cereal

One of L.A.'s Universal Studios attractions is a simulated 8.3 one of these

By itself, it's a gait; with "fox" or "turkey," it's a dance

In ice skating, examples of these include the lutz, the double lutz, and spread-eagled lutz

Your heart's right ventricle pumps blood only to this pair of organs

DOUBLE JEOPARDY!

EXPLORERS

Who was Ferdinand Magellan?

Who was Vasco Núñez de Balboa?

What is Africa?

Who was Prince Henry the Navigator?

What is Quebec?

FIRST LADIES

Who is Rosalynn Carter?

What is Mount Vernon?

Who was Dolley Madison? (ACC: Dolley Payne Todd)

Who is Jacqueline Kennedy?

Who was Mary Todd Lincoln?

EUROPE

What are the Pyrenees?

What is Austria?

What is the Warsaw Pact?

What are the Channel Islands?

What is Czechoslovakia?

NURSERY RHYMES	NUCLEAR PHYSICS	HODGEPODGE
What is the fair?	What is the nucleus?	Who is Cap'n Crunch?
"(Baa, baa, black sheep,) have you any wool?"	What are alpha, beta, and gamma?	What is an earthquake?
What is "lays eggs"?	What is uranium?	What is trot?
What is "What a good boy am I"?	What is 26?	What are jumps?
What is seven?	What is a meltdown?	What are the lungs?

FINAL JEOPARDY!

SOUTH AMERICA

This South American country is named for an Italian city

FINAL JEOPARDY!

SOUTH AMERICA

What is Venezuela?